SAY IT IN
HEBREW

BY

ALEEZA CERF BEARE

Second Revised Edition

DOVER PUBLICATIONS, INC.
NEW YORK

CONTENTS

INTRODUCTION

Say it in Hebrew makes available to you, in simple usable form, all the words and sentences you need for travel and everyday living in Israel. The English sentences and phrases given are those proven by experience to be the most needed. The translations are idiomatic rather than literal. In order to achieve correct pronunciation, all the Hebrew words are presented in a simple phonetic transcription, explained in the Scheme of Pronunciation on page 11.

SENTENCE STRUCTURE

No attempt is made in this book to teach Hebrew grammar. Almost every given phrase and sentence is complete in itself and can be used without a knowledge of grammar.

The plan of the book is designed to help you form additional sentences of your own. Thus for the words in square brackets you can substitute the words immediately following (in the same sentence or in the indented entries below). For example, the entry

I forgot [my money] my keys.

provides two sentences: "I forgot my money," and "I forgot my keys." Three sentences are provided by the entry

Here is my [baggage].
—— health certificate.
—— passport.

As your Hebrew vocabulary increases, you will find

that you can express an increasingly wide range of thoughts by the proper substitution of words in these model sentences.

GENDER

Do not be deterred from speaking Hebrew by the fact that you will undoubtedly make grammatical errors. A native listener will usually understand what you wish to say. When speaking Hebrew, however, you can avoid many errors by paying some attention to the gender of nouns. Gender in Hebrew is more complex than in English and Romance languages. Pronouns and verbs often change their forms or endings depending upon whether a male or female is speaking and sometimes when a male or female is addressed. *Say it in Hebrew* does not attempt to teach the complexities of gender inflection. However, it is presented so that simple substitutions can be made and mistakes avoided with an understanding of this problem. Hebrew is always written from right to left. All references to gender changes are enclosed in parentheses and the masculine form always precedes the feminine form in the Hebrew text and transcription.

The following table lists the scheme of abbreviations used to indicate necessary gender changes throughout the book.

M.	male speaking to anyone
F.	female speaking to anyone
M. TO F.	male speaking to female
F. TO M.	female speaking to male
TO M.	anyone speaking to male
TO F.	anyone speaking to female

If there is no indication of gender in the entry, the sentence can be used by either male or female speaking to male or female. It is applicable in any gender situation.

The following examples are given to specifically illustrate most situations requiring gender changes as outlined in the table above.

Example A. If the abbreviation M. or F. appears, the masculine form should be used when a male is speaking, and the feminine form should be used when a female is speaking.

> I am busy.
>
> אֲנִי (עָסוּק) (עֲסוּקָה).
>
> a-NEE (a-SOOK, M.) (a-soo-KAH, F.).

In the above sentence a man would say

> I am busy.
>
> אֲנִי עָסוּק.
>
> a-NEE a-SOOK, M.

but a woman would say

> I am busy.
>
> אֲנִי עֲסוּקָה.
>
> a-NEE a-soo-KAH, F.

Example B. If the abbreviation TO M. or TO F. appears, the masculine form should be used when a male is addressed and the feminine form should be used when a female is addressed.

What do you wish?

מַה (רְצוֹנְךָ) (רְצוֹנֵךְ)?

MAH (ruh-tson-KHAH, to m.) *(ruh-tson-AYKH,* to f.) ?

In the above sentence a male or female speaking to Bill Brown would say

> What do you wish?
>
> מַה רְצוֹנְךָ?
>
> *MAH ruh-tson-KHAH,* to m. ?

A male or female speaking to Jean Jones would say

> What do you wish?
>
> מַה רְצוֹנֵךְ?
>
> *MAH ruh-tson-AYKH,* to f. ?

Occasionally a sentence requires a change of gender for the speaker as well as that of the person addressed. This is indicated by the abbreviation M. TO F. or F. TO M.

THE INDEX

You will find the extensive index at the end of this book especially helpful. All the sentences, phrases and words are numbered from 1–1303. Numbers in the index refer you to each specific entry.

PRONUNCIATION

Say it in Hebrew follows the official pronunciation of modern Israeli Hebrew. The Sefardic pronunciation is used in this book because it is the colloquial speech of Israel today. When you travel in Israel, especially outside the capital, you will hear many dialectic differences in the native speech. But if you use this standard pronunciation, you will be understood everywhere.

Pronounce the phonetic transcriptions as though they were English text, with regard for those few Hebrew sounds that do not exist in English. These sounds have been marked with an arrow in the Scheme of Pronunciation to indicate that they need special attention. It is not necessary to memorize the Scheme of Pronunciation on the following page—though you will find it helpful to read through it until you are familiar with the Hebrew letters and the corresponding transcription. In the phonetic transcription accented or stressed syllables are written in capital letters. Try pronouncing half a dozen of the phrases, then check yourself by the table. You will soon find that you have learned the scheme and need not refer to it very frequently.

In the phonetic system, consistency and complete accuracy are sometimes sacrificed for simplicity and ease of comprehension. You are urged to use it only as a temporary guide; abandon it as soon as possible— that is as soon as you have mastered the pronunciation of the Hebrew letters. If you study in a class or with a private teacher, you may be asked to drop it to avoid confusion with other systems.

Most beginners greatly over-rate the task of learning Hebrew letters. The mastery of their pronunciation in reading is not difficult because there are less than 35 letters (consonants and vowels) and these usually have the same sound equivalents. The problem is not akin to learning how to read English with all its spelling and phonetic irregularities. Even if you do not go on to further study, you will be amply repaid for this effort by your ability to read proper names, street signs and other signs.

SCHEME OF PRONUNCIATION

Hebrew Letter	Transcription	Example
א	–	silent, like h in hour
ב	b	as in barn
ב	v	as in very
ג	g	as in gold, never as in gem
ד	d	as in dental
ה	h	as in horn, never silent
ו	v	as in very
ז	z	as in zone
ח	kh	No English equivalent. Like ch in Scottish loch or German Bach.
ט, ת	t	as in ten
י	y	as in yard
כ, ך	k	as in kite. Never silent as in knit
כ	kh	(see note on ח, above)
ל	l	as in let
מ, ם	m	as in met
נ, ן	n	as in net
ס	s	as in say
ע	–	silent, like h in hour
פ, ף	p	as in pay
פ	f	as in fit
צ, ץ	ts	as in lets
ק	k	as in kate

* This is the form of the letter when it appears at the end of a word.

11

Hebrew Letter	Transcription	Example
➔ ר	r	Produced by vibrating the uvula against the back of the tongue, as in French or German. A gargling *r* sound.
שׁ	sh	as in *sh*ell
שׂ	s	as in *s*ay
ת	t	as in *t*en

VOWEL SOUNDS

The vowels of Hebrew are indicated by means of diacritical marks written under the consonants they are to follow. In order to write a vowel, therefore, it is necessary to combine it with a consonant or silent letter from the alphabet given above. We have used א (A-leph) in the examples below, because it has no sound of its own.

Hebrew Vowel	Transcription	Example	Notes
אָ ,אַ ,אָ	ah (long)*	as in father	Length here refers to duration rather than quality. The short vowel is merely spoken more quickly.
אָ ,אֲ ,אַ	a (short)*	as in comma	
אֶ	e, or eh	as in met	In the transcription we have sometimes used *eh* for this sound to warn that it is not to be pronounced *ee*.
אֵ	ay	like *a* in date	A pure vowel and not a diphthong. Try to say *ay* without ending on the sound of *ee*.
אֵי	ay	as in day	

13

Hebrew Vowel	Transcription	Example	Notes
אֵ ,אֶ	ee	as in meet	
אֵי	ie	as in lie	A diphthong, i.e., a sound composed of two vowels: ah-ee.
אוֹ	oh (long)*	like oo in door	Length here refers to duration rather than quality. Notice how the sound is more drawn out in door.
אָ ,אֹו ,אֹ	o (short)*	like ou in ought	
אֹו ,אֻ	oo	as in food	Never as in book.
אְ	uh	like e in the	The very short, indistinct sound of e in the or sudden, as they are spoken in normal, rapid speech.

* The distinction between the pronunciation of the long and short vowel a (a and ah) and o (o and oh) is not phonemic in Hebrew. This distinction never affects the meaning of words. In modern spoken Hebrew such distinctions are becoming rather vague and haphazard. Although the transcription attempts to differentiate between long and short a and o, bear in mind that these differences are not consistent or important in modern spoken Hebrew.

THE HEBREW ALPHABET

The Hebrew alphabet is given below along with the pronunciation of each letter according to the transcription used in this book. You will find it useful in spelling out names and addresses.

Hebrew Letter	Pronunciation
א	A-lef
ב	bayt
ב	vayt
ג	GEE-mel
ד	DAH-let
ה	hay
ו	vahv
ז	ZAH-yeen
ח	khet
ט	tet
י	yood
כ	kaff
*ך כ	khaff
ל	LAH-med
*ם מ	mem
*ן נ	noon
ס	SAH-mekh
ע	AH-yeen
פ	pay
*ף פ	fay
*ץ צ	TSAH-dee

* This is the form of the letter when it appears at the end of a word.

15

Hebrew Letter	*Pronunciation*
ק	koof
ר	raysh
שׁ	sheen
שׂ	seen
ת	tav

GENERAL EXPRESSIONS

בְּסִמֵּי יוֹם־יוֹם

1. Yes.

כֵּן.

kayn.

כֵּן

2. No.

לֹא.

loh.

לֹא

3. Perhaps.

אוּלַי.

oo-LIE.

4. Please.

בְּבַקָּשָׁה.

buh-va-ka-SHAH.

5. Excuse me.

סְלִיחָה.

slee-KHAH.

סְלִיחָה

6. Thanks very much.

תּוֹדָה רַבָּה.

tuh-DAH ra-BAH.

תּוֹדָה

7. You are welcome. *lit.* It is nothing.

עַל לֹא דָּבָר.

al loh da-VAHR.

8. It is all right.

זֶה בְּסֵדֶר.

zeh buh-SAY-der.

9. It doesn't matter.

אֵין דָּבָר.

ayn da-VAHR.

10. That is all.

זֶה הַכֹּל.

zeh ha-KOL.

11. Wait a moment.

(חַכֵּה) (חַכִּי) רֶגַע.

(kha-KAY, TO M.) (kha-KEE, TO F.) REH-gah.

12. Come in !

יָבֹא!

ya-VOH!

13. Come here.

(בֹּא) (בֹּאִי) הֵנָּה.

(boh, TO M.) (BOH-ee, TO F.) HAY-na.

14. What do you wish?

מַה (רְצוֹנְךָ) (רְצוֹנֵךְ)?

MAH (ruh-tson-KHAH, TO M.) (ruh-tson-AYKH, TO F.) ?

15. What?

מַה?

mah?

16. Who?

מִי?

mee?

17. When?

מָתַי?

ma-TIE?

18. Where?

אֵיפֹה?

ay-FOH?

19. Why?

מַדּוּעַ?

ma-DOO-ah?

20. How long?

כַּמָּה זְמַן?

ka-MAH zman?

21. What is the distance?

מַה הַמֶּרְחָק?

mah ha-mehr-KHAK?

22. Listen.

(שְׁמַע) (שִׁמְעִי).

(shmah, TO M.*) (sheem-EE,* TO F.*).*

23. Careful!

זְהִירוּת!

zuh-hee-ROOT!

YOURSELF

פְּרָטִים אִישִׁיִּים

24. My name is ——.

שְׁמִי ——.

shmee ——.

25. My name is spelled ——.

כּוֹתְבִים אֶת שְׁמִי ——.

kot-VEEM et shmee ——.

26. I am 25 years old.

אֲנִי (בֶּן, m.) (בַּת, f.) עֶשְׂרִים וְחָמֵשׁ.

a-NEE (ben, M.) (bat, F.) es-REEM vuh-khah-MAYSH.

27. I am an American citizen.

אֲנִי תּוֹשָׁב אֲמֶרִיקָאִי.

a-NEE toh-SHAHV a-me-ree-KAH-ee.

28. My address is ——.

כְּתָבְתִּי הִיא ——.

kuh-tov-TEE hee ——.

29. I am a student.

אֲנִי (תַּלְמִיד) (תַּלְמִידָה).

a-NEE (tal-MEED, M.) (tal-mee-DAH, F).

30. A teacher.

(מוֹרֶה) (מוֹרָה).

(moh-REH, M.) (moh-RAH, F.).

31. A business man.

אִישׁ מִסְחָר.

eesh mees-KHAR.

32. I am a friend of ——.

אֲנִי (יָדִיד) (יְדִידָה) שֶׁל——.

a-NEE (yuh-DEED, M.) (yuh-dee-DAH, F.) shel——.

33. I have come here on [a business trip].

בָּאתִי הֵנָּה לְשֵׁם [מִסְחָר].

BAH-tee HAY-nah luh-SHAYM [mees-KHAR].

34. —— a vacation.

חֹפֶשׁ.

KHO-fesh.

35. I am traveling to ——.

אֲנִי (נוֹסֵעַ) (נוֹסַעַת) לְ——.

a-NEE (noh-SAY-ah, M.) (noh-SAH-at, F.) luh——.

36. I am [warm] cold.

[חַם] קַר לִי.

[KHAM] KAHR lee.

37. I am busy.

אֲנִי (עָסוּק) (עֲסוּקָה).

a-NEE (a-SOOK, M.) (a-soo-KAH, F.).

38. I am glad.

אֲנִי (שָׂמֵחַ) (שְׂמֵחָה).

a-NEE (sa-MAY-akh, M.) (smay-KHAH, F.).

39. I am tired.

אֲנִי (עָיֵף) (עֲיֵפָה).

a-NEE (a-YAYF, M.) (a-yay-FAH, F.).

40. I am sorry.

צַר לִי.

TSAHR lee.

41. I am in a hurry.

אֲנִי (מְמַהֵר) (מְמַהֶרֶת).

a-NEE (muh-mah-HAYR, M.) (muh-mah-HEH-ret, F.).

42. I am ready.

אֲנִי (מוּכָן) (מוּכָנָה).

a-NEE (moo-KHAN, M.) (moo-kha-NAH, F.).

43. I am hungry.

אֲנִי (רָעֵב) (רְעֵבָה).

a-NEE (rah-AYV, M.) (ruh-ay-VAH, F.).

44. I am thirsty.

אֲנִי (צָמֵא) (צְמֵאָה).

a-NEE (tsah-MAY, M.) (tsmay-AH, F.).

GREETINGS AND SOCIAL CONVERSATION

בְּרָכוֹת, עֲשִׂיַּת הַכָּרָה, וְכוּ׳

45. Good morning.

בֹּקֶר טוֹב.

BO-kehr tov.

46. Good evening.

עֶרֶב טוֹב.

EH-rev tov.

47. Hello.

שָׁלוֹם.

sha-LOM.

48. Good-bye.

לְהִתְרָאוֹת *or* שָׁלוֹם.

luh-heet-ra-OT or sha-LOM.

49. How are you?

מַה (שְׁלוֹמְךָ) (שְׁלוֹמֵךְ)

MAH (shlom-KHAH, TO M.) (shlo-MAYKH, TO. F)?

50. Fine thanks, and you?

טוֹב תּוֹדָה, (וְאַתָּה) (וְאַתְּ)

tov toh-DAH, (vuh-a-TAH, TO M.) (vuh-AT, TO F.)?

51. How is the family?

מַה שְׁלוֹם הַמִּשְׁפָּחָה?

MAH shlom ha-meesh-pa-KHAH?

52. Very well.

טוֹב מְאֹד.

TOV muh-OD.

53. Not very well.

לֹא כָּל כָּךְ טוֹב.

loh kol kakh TOV.

54. How are things?

מַה נִּשְׁמָע?

MAH neesh-MAH?

55. All right.

הַכֹּל בְּסֵדֶר.

ha-KOHL buh-SEH-dehr.

56. So, so.

כָּכָה כָּכָה.

KA-kha, KA-kha.

57. May I introduce [Mr. ——].

נָא לְהַכִּיר אֶת [אָדוֹן ——].

NAH luh-ha-KEER et [a-DON ——].

58. —— Miss or Mrs. ——.

גְּבֶרֶת ——.

guh-VEH-ret ——.

59. —— my wife.

אִשְׁתִּי.

eesh-TEE.

60. —— my husband.

בַּעֲלִי.

bah-ah-LEE.

61. —— my daughter.

בִּתִּי.

bee-TEE.

62. —— my son.

בְּנִי.

buh-NEE.

63. —— my sister.

אֲחוֹתִי.

a-kho-TEE.

64. —— my brother.

אָחִי.

a-KHEE.

65. —— my mother.

אִמִּי.

ee-MEE.

66. —— my father.

אָבִי.

a-VEE.

67. —— my friend.

(חֲבֵרִי) (חֲבֶרְתִּי).

(kha-veh-REE, M.) (kha-vehr-TEE, F.).

68. I am glad to meet you.

נָעִים לְהַכִּיר (אוֹתְךָ) (אוֹתָךְ).

na-EEM luh-ha-KEER (ot-KHAH, TO M.) (o-TAKH, TO F.).

69. What is your name, please?

מַה (שִׁמְךָ) (שְׁמֵךְ) בְּבַקָּשָׁה?

mah (sheem-KHAH, TO M.) (SHMAYKH, TO F.) buh-va-ka-SHAH?

70. Will you join us?

הַאִם (תִּצְטָרֵף) (תִּצְטָרְפִי) אֵלֵינוּ

ha-EEM (teets-ta-RAYF, TO M.) (teets-tar-FEE, F.).
e-LAY-noo?

71. Please sit down.

נָא לָשֶׁבֶת.

nah la-SHEH-vet.

72. Who is [this boy]?

מִי הוּא [הַיֶּלֶד הַזֶּה]?

mee hoo [ha-YEH-led ha-ZEH]?

73. —— this man.

הָאִישׁ הַזֶּה.

ha-EESH ha-ZEH.

74. Who is [this girl]?

מִי הִיא [הַיַּלְדָּה הַזֹּאת]?

mee hee [ha-yal-DAH ha-ZOT]?

75. —— this woman.

הָאִשָּׁה הַזֹּאת.

ha-ee-SHAH ha-ZOT.

76. May I have your address?

הַאוּכַל לְקַבֵּל אֶת (כְּתָבְתְּךָ) (כְּתָבְתֵּךְ)?

ha-oo-KHAL luh-ka-BAYL et (ktov-teh-KHAH, TO M.)
(ktov-TAYKH, TO F.)?

77. Your telephone number.

אֶת מִסְפַּר הַטֶּלֶפוֹן (שֶׁלְּךָ) (שֶׁלָּךְ).

et mees-PAHR ha-teh-leh-FON (shel-KHAH, TO M.)
(sheh-LAKH, TO F.).

78. What are you doing tonight?

מָה (אַתָּה עוֹשֶׂה) (אַתְּ עוֹשָׂה) הָעֶרֶב?

mah (a-TAH o-SEH, TO M.) (at o-SAH, TO F.) ha-EH-rev?

79. May I call on you again?

הַאִם אוּכַל לְבַקֵּר (אוֹתְךָ) (אוֹתָךְ) שׁוּב?

ha-EEM oo-KHAL luh-va-KAYR (ot-KHAH, TO M.) (o-TAKH, TO F.) shoov?

80. I have enjoyed myself very much.

נֶהֱנֵיתִי מְאֹד.

neh-heh-NAY-tee muh-OD.

81. I had a very good time.

בִּלִּיתִי יָפֶה מְאֹד.

bee-LEE-tee ya-FEH muh-OD.

82. Come to see us.

(בּוֹא) (בּוֹאִי) לְבַקֵּר אוֹתָנוּ.

(boh, TO M.) (BOH-ee, TO F.) luh-va-KAYR o-TAH-noo.

83. I like you very much.

(אַתָּה מוֹצֵא) (אַתְּ מוֹצֵאת) חֵן בְּעֵינַי מְאֹד.

(a-TAH mo-TSAY, TO M.) (at mo-TSAYT, TO F.) khayn buh-ay-NIE muh-OD.

84. I love you.

אֲנִי (אוֹהֵב אוֹתְךָ) (אוֹהֶבֶת אוֹתְךָ).

a-NEE (o-HAYV o-TAKH, M. TO F.) (o-HEH-vet ot-KHAH, F. TO M.).

MAKING YOURSELF UNDERSTOOD

לְהָבָנָה הַדָּדִית

85. Do you speak English?

הַאִם (אַתָּה מְדַבֵּר) (אַתְּ מְדַבֶּרֶת) אַנְגְּלִית?

ha-EEM (a-TAH muh-da-BAYR, TO M.) (at muh-da-BEH-ret, TO F.) ang-LEET?

86. Does anyone here speak English?

הַאִם מִישֶׁהוּ פֹּה מְדַבֵּר אַנְגְּלִית?

ha-EEM MEE-sheh-hoo poh muh-da-BAYR ang-LEET?

86a. I speak only English.

אֲנִי (מְדַבֵּר) (מְדַבֶּרֶת) רַק אַנְגְּלִית.

a-NEE (muh-da-BAYR, M.) (muh-da-BEH-ret, F.) rak ang-LEET.

87. I know a little Hebrew.

אֲנִי (מְדַבֵּר) (מְדַבֶּרֶת) קְצָת עִבְרִית.

a-NEE (muh-da-BAYR, M.) (muh-da-BEH-ret, F.) ktsat eev-REET.

88. Yiddish.

אִידִישׁ.

EE-deesh.

89. German.

גֶּרְמָנִית.

gehr-ma-NEET.

90. French.

צָרְפָתִית.

tsor-fa-TEET.

91. Please speak more slowly.

נָא לְדַבֵּר יוֹתֵר לְאַט.

nah luh-da-BAYR yo-TAYR luh-AT.

92. I do not understand.

אֵינֶנִּי (מֵבִין) (מְבִינָה).

ay-NEH-nee (may-VEEN, M.) (muh-vee-NAH, F.).

93. Do you understand me?

הַאִם (אַתָּה מֵבִין) (אַתְּ מְבִינָה) אוֹתִי?

ha-EEM (a-TAH may-VEEN, TO M.) (at muh-vee-NAH, TO F.) o-TEE?

94. I don't know.

אֵינֶנִּי (יוֹדֵעַ) (יוֹדַעַת).

ay-NEH-nee (yo-DAY-a, M.) (yo-DAH-at, F.).

95. I don't think so.

אֵינֶנִּי (סָבוּר) (סְבוּרָה) כָּךְ.

ay-NEH-nee (sa-VOOR, M.) (svoo-RAH, F.) kakh.

96. Repeat it, please.

נָא לַחֲזוֹר עַל זֶה.

nah la-kha-ZOR al zeh.

97. What is that?

מַה זֶה?

mah zeh?

98. What does that mean?

מַה זֹּאת אוֹמֶרֶת?

mah zot o-MEH-ret?

99. How do you say "———" in Hebrew?

אֵיךְ אוֹמְרִים «———» בְּעִבְרִית?

aykh om-REEM "———" buh-eev-REET?

100. How do you spell "———"?

אֵיךְ כּוֹתְבִים «———»?

aykh kot-VEEM "———"?

101. We need an interpreter.

נָחוּץ לָנוּ תֻּרְגְּמָן.

na-KHOOTS LAH-noo toor-guh-MAN.

DIFFICULTIES

קָשָׁיִים

102. Where is [the American Consulate]?

אֵיפֹה [הַקּוֹנְסוּלְיָה הָאֲמֵרִיקָאִית]?

ay-FOH [ha-kon-SOOL-ya ha-a-meh-ree-KAH-eet]?

103. ——— the police station.

תַּחֲנַת הַמִּשְׁטָרָה.

ta-kha-NAT ha-meesh-ta-RAH.

104. ——— the lost and found office.

מַחְלֶקֶת אֲבֵדוֹת וּמְצִיאוֹת.

makh-LEH-ket a-vay-DOT oo-muh-tsee-OT.

105. ——— the rest room *or* the toilet.

בֵּית הַשִּׁמּוּשׁ.

bayt ha-shee-MOOSH.

106. Can you help me?

(הַתּוּכַל) (הַתּוּכְלִי) לַעֲזוֹר לִי?

(ha-too-KHAL, TO M.*) (ha-tookh-LEE,* TO F.*) la-a-ZOR lee?*

107. Can you tell me?

(הַתּוּכַל) (הַתּוּכְלִי) לוֹמַר לִי?

(ha-too-KHAL, TO M.*) (ha-tookh-LEE,* TO F.*) loh-MAHR lee?*

108. I am looking for my friends.

אֲנִי (מְחַפֵּשׂ) (מְחַפֶּשֶׂת) אֶת חֲבֵרַי.

a-NEE (muh-kha-PAYS, M.) (muh-kha-PEH-set, F.)
et kha-vay-RIE.

109. I cannot find my hotel.

אֵינֶנִּי (יָכוֹל) (יְכוֹלָה) לִמְצֹא אֶת הַמָּלוֹן שֶׁלִּי.

ay-NEH-nee (ya-KHOL, M.) (yuh-kho-LAH, F.)
leem-TSOH et ha-ma-LON sheh-LEE.

110. I do not remember the number.

אֵינֶנִּי (זוֹכֵר) (זוֹכֶרֶת) אֶת הַמִּסְפָּר.

ay-NEH-nee (zoh-KHAYR, M.) (zoh-KHEH-ret, F.)
et ha-mees-PAHR.

111. The street.

אֶת הָרְחוֹב.

et ha-ruh-KHOV.

112. I have lost my purse.

אִבַּדְתִּי אֶת הָאַרְנָק שֶׁלִּי.

ee-BA-duh-tee et ha-ar-NAK sheh-LEE.

113. It is not my fault.

זוֹ לֹא אַשְׁמָתִי.

zoo loh ash-ma-TEE.

114. I forgot [my money] my keys.

שָׁכַחְתִּי [אֶת כַּסְפִּי] אֶת מַפְתְּחוֹתַי.

sha-KHAKH-tee [et kas-PEE] et maf-tuh-kho-TIE.

115. I have missed the train.

אֵחַרְתִּי אֶת הָרַכֶּבֶת.

eh-KHAR-tee et ha-ra-KEH-vet.

116. What am I to do?

מַה עָלַי לַעֲשׂוֹת?

meh a-LIE la-a-SOT?

117. Where are we going?

לְאָן אֲנַחְנוּ הוֹלְכִים?

luh-AN a-NAKH-noo hol-KHEEM?

118. Go away.

(לֵךְ מִפֹּה) (לְכִי מִפֹּה).

(LEHKH mee-poh, TO M.) (luh-KHEE mee-poh, TO F.).

119. I will call a policeman.

אֶקְרָא לְשׁוֹטֵר.

ek-RAH luh-sho-TAYR.

120. My money has been stolen.

גָּנְבוּ לִי אֶת כַּסְפִּי.

gan-VOO lee et kas-PEE.

121. Help!

הַצִּילוּ!

ha-TSEE-loo!

122. Fire!

שְׂרֵפָה!

sray-FAH!

123. Thief!

גַּנָּב!

ga-NAHV!

CUSTOMS

מֶכֶס

124. Where is the customs?

אֵיפֹה הַמֶּכֶס?

ay-FOH ha-MEH-khes?

125. Here is my [baggage].

הִנֵּה [הַמִּזְוָדוֹת] שֶׁלִּי.

hee-NEH [ha-meez-va-DOT] sheh-LEE.

126. —— health certificate.

תְּעוּדַת בְּרִיאוּת.

tuh-oo-DAT bree-OOT.

127. —— identification.

תְּעוּדַת זֶהוּת.

tuh-oo-DAT zeh-HOOT.

128. —— passport.

דַּרְכּוֹן.

dar-KON.

129. In this suitcase I have gifts.

בְּמִזְוָדָה זוֹ יֵשׁ לִי מַתָּנוֹת.

buh-meez-va-DAH zoo yesh lee ma-ta-NOT.

130. The five pieces [to your left] to your right are mine.

חֲמֵשֶׁת הַחֲתִיכוֹת [לִשְׂמֹאלְךָ] לִימִינְךָ הֵן שֶׁלִּי.

kha-MEH-shet ha-kha-tee-KHOT [luh-smol-KHAH] lee-meen-KHAH hayn sheh-LEE.

131. I cannot find all my baggage.

אֵינֶנִּי (יָכֹל) (יְכוֹלָה) לִמְצֹא אֶת כָּל הַמִּזְוָדוֹת שֶׁלִּי.

*ay-NEH-nee (ya-KHOL, M.) (yuh-kho-LAH, F.)
leem-TSOH et kol ha-meez-va-DOT sheh-LEE.*

132. I have nothing to declare.

אֵין לִי מַה לְהַצְהִיר.

ayn lee mah luh-hats-HEER.

133. I have something to declare.

יֵשׁ לִי מַה לְהַצְהִיר.

yesh lee mah luh-hats-HEER.

134. Must I open everything?

הַאִם עָלַי לִפְתֹּחַ אֶת הַכֹּל?

ha-EEM a-LIE leef-TO-akh et ha-KOL?

135. I cannot open the suitcase.

אֵינֶנִּי (יָכֹל) (יְכוֹלָה) לִפְתֹּחַ אֶת הַמִּזְוָדָה.

ay-NEH-nee (ya-KHOL, M.) (yuh-kho-LAH, F.) leef-TO-akh et ha-meez-va-DAH.

136. All this is for my personal use.

כָּל אֵלֶּה הֵם צָרְכַי הַפְּרָטִיִּים.

kol AY-leh haym tsra-KHIE ha-pra-tee-EEM.

137. There is nothing here but clothing.

אֵין פֹּה דָּבָר חוּץ מִבְּנָדִים.

ayn poh da-VAHR khoots mee-buh-ga-DEEM.

138. Are these things dutiable?

הַאִם חֲפָצִים אֵלֶּה חַיָּבִים מֶכֶס?

ha-EEM kha-fa-TSEEM AY-leh kha-ya-VEEM MEH-khes?

139. That is all I have.

זֶה כָּל מַה שֶּׁיֵּשׁ לִי.

zeh kol mah sheh-YESH lee.

140. How much must I pay?

כַּמָּה עָלַי לְשַׁלֵּם?

ka-MAH a-LIE leh-sha-LAYM?

141. Have you finished?

הַאִם גָּמַרְתָּ?

ha-EEM ga-MAR-ta?

BAGGAGE

מִטְעָן

142. I want to leave these bags here for a few days.

אֲנִי (רוֹצֶה) (רוֹצָה) לְהַשְׁאִיר פֹּה אֶת הַמִּזְוָדוֹת הָאֵלּוּ לְכַמָּה יָמִים.

a-NEE (ro-TSEH, M.) (ro-TSAH, F.) luh-hash-
EER poh et ha-meez-va-DOT ha-AY-loo luh-kha-
MAH ya-MEEM.

143. Where is the baggage checked?

אֵיפֹה מוֹסְרִים אֶת הַמִּטְעָן?

ay-FOH mos-REEM et ha-meet-AN?

144. The receipt.

הַקַּבָּלָה.

ha-ka-ba-LAH.

145. The number.

הַמִּסְפָּר.

ha-mees-PAHR.

146. The baggage room.

מַחְסַן הַמִּטְעָן.

makh-SAN ha-meet-AN.

147. Can I check my baggage through to ——?

הַאוּכַל לִשְׁלֹחַ אֶת חֲפָצַי יָשָׁר לְ——?

ha-oo-KHAL leesh-LOH-akh et kha-fa-TSIE ya-
SHAHR luh——?

148. I have come to take out my baggage.

בָּאתִי לְקַבֵּל אֶת חֲפָצַי.

BA-tee luh-ka-BAYL et kha-fa-TSIE.

149. Where can I find a porter?

אֵיפֹה אֶמְצָא סַבָּל?

ay-FOH em-TSA sa-BAL?

150. What is your number?

מַה מִּסְפָּרְךָ?

mah mees-pahr-KHAH?

151. Follow me, please.

נָא לָבֹא אִתִּי.

nah la-VOH ee-TEE.

152. Handle this carefully, please.

נָא לְהִזָּהֵר עִם זֶה.

na luh-hee-za-HAYR eem zeh.

153. Put it all in a taxi.

(שִׂים) אֶת הַכֹּל בְּטַקְסִי.

(seem, TO M.) et ha-KOL buh-TAK-see.

TRAVEL: DIRECTIONS

נְסִיעָה: כִּוּוּנִים

154. Can you recommend a travel agent?

(הֲתוּכַל) (הֲתוּכְלִי) לְהַמְלִיץ עַל סוֹכֵן נְסִיעוֹת?

(ha-too-KHAL, TO M.) (ha-tookh-LEE, TO F.) luh-ham-LEETS al so-KHAYN nuh-see-OHT?

155. Travel agency.

סוֹכְנוּת נְסִיעוֹת.

sokkh-NOOT nuh-see-OHT.

156. I want to go [to the airline office] to the government tourist office.

בִּרְצוֹנִי לָלֶכֶת [לְמִשְׂרַד הַתְּעוּפָה] לְמִשְׂרַד הַתַּיָּרוּת
הַמֶּמְשַׁלְתִּי.

beer-tso-NEE la-LEH-khet [luh-mees-RAD ha-tuh-
oo-FAH] luh-mees-RAD ha-ta-ya-ROOT ha-mem-
shal-TEE.

157. Is the bus stop nearby?

הַאִם תַּחֲנַת הָאוֹטוֹבּוּסִים קְרוֹבָה לְכַאן?

ha-EEM ta-kha-NAT ha-o-to-BOO-seem kro-VAH
leh-KHAHN?

158. How long will it take to go to the airport?

כַּמָּה זְמַן לוֹקַחַת הַנְּסִיעָה לִשְׂדֵה הַתְּעוּפָה?

ka-MAH zman lo-KA-khat ha-nuh-see-AH lees-DAY
ha-tuh-oo-FAH?

159. When will we arrive at ——?

מָתַי נַגִּיעַ לְ——?

ma-TIE na-GEE-a luh——?

160. Is this the direct way to ——?

הַאִם זוֹ הַדֶּרֶךְ הַיְשִׁירָה לְ——?

ha-EEM zoo ha-DEH-rekh ha-yuh-shee-RAH luh-
——?

161. Please tell me the way [to the business section].

נָא לְהַגִּיד לִי אֶת הַדֶּרֶךְ [לָרֹבַע הַמִּסְחָרִי].

nah luh-ha-GEED lee et ha-DEH-rekh [la-ROH-va
ha-mees-kha-REE].

162. —— to the shops.

לַחֲנֻיּוֹת.

la-kha-noo-YOT.

163. —— to the residential section.

לְרֹבַע הַמְגוּרִים.

luh-ROH-va ham-goo-REEM.

164. Should I turn [to the east]?

הַאִם עָלַי לִפְנוֹת [מִזְרָחָה]?

ha-EEM a-LIE leef-NOT [meez-RA-kha]?

165. —— to the west.

מַעֲרָבָה.

ma-a-RA-va.

166. —— to the north.

צָפוֹנָה.

tsa-FO-na.

167. —— to the south.

דְּרוֹמָה.

da-RO-ma.

168. —— to the right.

יְמִינָה.

yeh-MEE-na,

169. —— to the left.

שְׂמֹאלָה.

SMO-la.

170. —— at the traffic light.

עַל יַד הָרַמְזוֹר.

al yad ha-rahm-ZOHR.

171. It is [on this side of the street], isn't it?

זֶה [בַּצַּד הַזֶּה שֶׁל הָרְחוֹב], לֹא כֵן?

zeh [ba-TSAD ha-ZEH shel ha-ruh-KHOV], lo khen?

172. —— on the other side of the boulevard.

בַּצַּד הָאַחֵר שֶׁל הַשְּׂדֵרָה.

ba-TSAD ha-a-KHAYR shel hash-day-RAH.

173. —— at the corner.

בַּפִּנָּה.

ba-pee-NAH.

174. —— across the bridge.

מֵעֵבֶר לַגֶּשֶׁר.

may-E-ver la-GEH-shehr.

175. —— inside the station.

בַּתַּחֲנָה.

ba-ta-kha-NAH.

176. —— outside the building.

מִחוּץ לַבִּנְיָן.

mee-KHOOTS la-been-YAN.

177. —— opposite the city hall.

מוּל הָעִירִיָּה.

MOOL ha-ee-ree-YAH.

178. —— beside the café.

עַל יַד בֵּית הַקָּפֶה.

al yad bayt ha-ka-FEH.

179. —— in front of the house.

לִפְנֵי הַבַּיִת.

leef-NAY ha-BAH-yeet.

180. —— behind the school.

מֵאֲחוֹרֵי בֵּית הַסֵּפֶר.

may-a-kho-RAY bayt ha-SAY-fehr.

181. —— straight ahead from the square.

יָשָׁר מֵהַכִּכָּר.

ya-SHAHR may-ha-kee-KAHR.

182. —— in the middle of the circle.

בְּאֶמְצַע הַמַּעְגָּל.

beh-EM-tsa ha-ma-a-GAL.

183. —— forward.

קָדִימָה.

ka-DEE-ma.

184. —— back.

חֲזָרָה.

kha-za-RAH.

185. —— in this direction.

בְּכִוּוּן זֶה.

buh-khee-VOON zeh.

186. Is it near?

הַאִם זֶה קָרוֹב?

ha-EEM zeh ka-ROV?

187. What is the distance?

מַה הַמֶּרְחָק?

mah ha-mehr-KHAK?

188. How does one go there?

אֵיךְ הוֹלְכִים לְשָׁם?

aykh hol-KHEEM luh-sham?

189. Can I walk there?

הַאוּכַל לָלֶכֶת לְשָׁם בָּרֶגֶל?

ha-oo-KHAL la-LEH-khet luh-sham ba-REH-gel?

190. Which is the fastest way?

מַהִי הַדֶּרֶךְ הַמְּהִירָה בְּיוֹתֵר?

MAH-hee ha-DEH-rekh ham-hee-RAH buh-yo-TAYR?

191. Am I going in the right direction?

הַאִם אֲנִי (הוֹלֵךְ) (הוֹלֶכֶת) בַּכִּוּוּן הַנָּכוֹן?

ha-EEM a-NEE (ho-LAYKH M.) *(ho-LEH-khet,* F.) *ba-kee-VOON ha-na-KHON?*

TICKETS

כַּרְטִיסִים

192. Where is [the ticket office]?

אֵיפֹה [הַקֻּפָּה]?

ay-FOH [ha-koo-PAH]?

193. —— the waiting room.

חֲדַר הַהַמְתָּנָה.

kha-DAHR ha-ham-ta-NAH.

194. —— the information bureau.

מִשְׂרַד הַמּוֹדִיעִין.

mees-RAD ha-mo-dee-EEN.

195. How much is a [one-way] ticket to ——?

כַּמָּה עוֹלֶה כַּרְטִיס [לִנְסִיעָה אַחַת] לְ——?

ka-MAH o-LEH kar-TEES [leen-see-AH a-KHAT] luh——?

196. —— round trip.

הָלוֹךְ וְחָזוֹר.

ha-LOKH vuh-kha-ZOR.

197. I want [a ticket].

אֲבַקֵשׁ [כַּרְטִיס].

a-va-KAYSH [kar-TEES].

198. —— a front seat.

מָקוֹם קִדְמִי.

ma-KOM keed-MEE.

199. —— a seat near the window.

מָקוֹם עַל יַד הַחַלּוֹן.

ma-KOM al yad ha-kha-LON.

200. —— a reserved seat.

מָקוֹם שָׁמוּר.

ma-KOM sha-MOOR.

201. —— a timetable.

לוּחַ נְסִיעוֹת.

LOO-akh nuh-see-OT.

202. I want to go [first class] second class.

בִּרְצוֹנִי לִנְסוֹעַ [בְּמַחְלָקָה רִאשׁוֹנָה] בְּמַחְלָקָה שְׁנִיָּה.

beer-tso-NEE leen-SO-a [buh-makh-luh-KAH ree-sho-NAH] buh-makh-luh-KAH shnee-YAH.

203. Can I get something to eat on this trip?

הַאוּכַל לְקַבֵּל מַשֶּׁהוּ לֶאֱכֹל בַּדֶּרֶךְ?

ha-oo-KHAL luh-ka-BAYL MAH-sheh-hoo leh-eh-KHOL ba-DEH-rekh?

204. May I stop at —— on the way?

הַאוּכַל לִשְׁהוֹת בְּ—— בַּדֶּרֶךְ?

ha-oo-KHAL leesh-HOT buh—— ba-DEH-rekh?

205. Can I go by way of ——?

הַאוּכַל לִנְסֹעַ דֶּרֶךְ

ha-oo-KHAL leen-SO-a DEH-rekh ——?

206. How long is this ticket good for?

לְכַמָּה זְמַן יָפֶה כֹּחוֹ שֶׁל כַּרְטִיס זֶה?

le-kha-MAH zman ya-FEH ko-KHOH shel kar-TEES zeh?

207. How many valises may I take?

כַּמָּה מְזָוָדוֹת אוּכַל לָקַחַת?

ka-MAH meez-va-DOT oo-KHAL la-KA-khat?

AIRPLANE

אֲוִירוֹן

208. Is there bus service to the airport?

הַאִם יֵשׁ שֵׁרוּת אוֹטוֹבּוּסִים לִשְׂדֵה הַתְּעוּפָה?

ha-EEM yesh shay-ROOT o-to-BOO-seem lees-DAY ha-tuh-oo-FAH?

209. When is there a plane to ——?

מָתַי יוֹצֵא אֲוִירוֹן לְ——?

ma-TIE yo-TSAY a-vee-RON luh——?

210. What is the flight number?

מַה מִסְפַּר הַטִּיסָה?

mah mees-PAHR ha-ee-SAH?

211. I have a confirmed reservation.

יֵשׁ לִי הַזְמָנָה מְאֻשֶּׁרֶת.

yesh lee haz-ma-NAH muh-oo-SHEH-ret.

212. Is food served on the plane?

הַאִם יַגִּישׁוּ אֹכֶל בָּאֲוִירוֹן?

ha-EEM ya-GEE-shoo O-khel ba-a-vee-RON?

213. How many kilos may I take?

כַּמָּה קִילוֹ מֻתָּר לִי לָקַחַת?

ka-MAH KEE-lo moo-TAHR lee la-KA-khat?

214. How much per kilo for excess baggage?

כַּמָּה עוֹלֶה הַקִּילוֹ מֵעַל לַמִּשְׁקָל הַמֻּתָּר?

ka-MAH o-LEH ha-KEE-lo may-AL la-meesh-KAL ha-moo-TAHR?

BOAT

אֳנִיָּה

215. Bon voyage!

נְסִיעָה טוֹבָה!

nuh-see-AH to-VAH!

216. All aboard please!

לַעֲלוֹת בְּבַקָּשָׁה!

la-a-LOT buh-va-ka-SHAH!

217. Is it time to go on board?

הַאִם הִגִּיעַ הַזְּמַן לַעֲלוֹת עַל הָאֳנִיָּה?

ha-EEM hee-GEE-a ha-zman la-a-LOT al ha-o-nee-YAH?

218. When does the next boat leave?

מָתַי תַּפְלִיג הָאֳנִיָּה הַבָּאָה?

ma-TIE taf-LEEG ha-o-nee-YAH ha-ba-AH?

219. Can I land at —— ?

הַאוּכַל לָרֶדֶת בְּ——?

ha-oo-KHAL la-REH-det buh——?

220. Please prepare my berth.

אֲבַקֵשׁ לַעֲשׂוֹת אֶת מִטָּתִי.

a-va-KAYSH la-a-SOT et mee-ta-TEE.

221. Please open [the porthole] the ventilator.

אֲבַקֵשׁ לִפְתּוֹחַ [אֶת הַחַלּוֹן] אֶת הַמְאַוְרֵר.

a-va-KAYSH leef-TO-akh [et ha-kha-LON] et ha-muh-av-RAYR.

222. I want to rent a deck chair.

בִּרְצוֹנִי לִשְׂכּוֹר כִּסֵּא מַרְגּוֹעַ.

beer-tso-NEE lees-KOR kee-SAY mar-GO-a.

223. Where can I find [the purser]?

אֵיפֹה אֶמְצָא אֶת [הַגִּזְבָּר]?

ay-FOH em-TSA et [ha-geez-BAHR]?

224. —— the steward.

הַמֶּלְצַר.

ha-mel-TSAHR.

225. —— the cabin steward.

מֶלְצַר הַתָּא.

mel-TSAHR ha-TAH.

226. —— the captain.

רַב הַחוֹבֵל.

rav ha-kho-VAYL.

227. I am going to my cabin.

אֲנִי (הוֹלֵךְ) (הוֹלֶכֶת) לַתָּא שֶׁלִּי.

a-NEE (ho-LAYKH, м.) (ho-LEH-khet, ғ.) la-TAH sheh-LEE.

228. To the upper deck.

לַסִפּוּן הָעֶלְיוֹן.

la-see-POON ha-el-YON.

229. To the lower deck.

לַסִפּוּן הַתַּחְתּוֹן.

la-see-POON ha-takh-TON.

230. To the dock.

לַנָּמֵל.

la-na-MAL.

231. I feel seasick.

יֵשׁ לִי מַחֲלַת יָם.

yesh lee ma-kha-LAT yam.

232. Do you have some dramamine?

הַאִם יֵשׁ (לְךָ) (לָךְ) דְּרָמָמִין?

he-EEM yesh (luh-KHAH, TO M.*) (lakh,* TO F.*)
dra-ma-MEEN?*

233. The life boat.

סִירַת הַהַצָּלָה.

see-RAT ha-ha-tsa-LAH.

234. The life preserver.

חֲגוֹרַת הַהַצָּלָה.

kha-go-RAT ha-ha-tsu-LAH.

TRAIN

רַכֶּבֶת

235. The arrival.

הַהַגָּעָה.

ha-ha-ga-AH.

236. The departure.

הַיְצִיאָה.

ha-yuh-tsee-AH.

237. Where is the railroad station?

אֵיפֹה תַּחֲנַת הָרַכֶּבֶת?

ay-FOH ta-kha-NAT ha-ra-KEH-vet?

238. When does the train leave for ——?

מָתַי יוֹצֵאת הָרַכֶּבֶת לְ——?

ma-TIE yo-TSAYT ha-ra-KEH-vet luh——?

239. Is the train from —— [late] on time?

הַאִם הָרַכֶּבֶת מִ—— [תִּתְאַחֵר] תַּגִּיעַ בִּזְמַן?

ha-EEM ha-ra-KEH-vet mee—— [teet-a-KHAYR] ta-GEE-a beez-MAN?

240. My train leaves in ten minutes.

הָרַכֶּבֶת שֶׁלִּי תֵּצֵא בְּעוֹד עֲשָׂרָה רְגָעִים.

ha-ra-KEH-vet sheh-LEE teh-TSAY buh-OD a-sa-RAH ruh-ga-EEM.

241. Does the train stop at ——?

הַאִם הָרַכֶּבֶת תַּעֲמֹד בְּ——?

ha-EEM ha-ra-KEH-vet ta-a-MOD buh——?

242. How long does the train stop at ——?

כַּמָּה זְמַן תַּעֲמֹד הָרַכֶּבֶת בְּ——?

ka-MAH zman ta-a-MOD ha-ra-KEH-vet buh——?

243. Is there an [earlier] later train?

הַאִם יֵשׁ רַכֶּבֶת [יוֹתֵר מוּקְדָּם] יוֹתֵר מְאֻחָר?

ha-EEM yesh ra-KEH-vet [yo-TAYR mook-DAM] yo-TAYR muh-oo-KHAHR?

244. Please [close] open the window.

נָא [לִסְגּוֹר] לִפְתּוֹחַ אֶת הַחַלּוֹן.

nah [lees-GOR] leef-TO-akh et ha-kha-LON.

245. Where is the [dining car]?

אֵיפֹה [קְרוֹן הַמִּסְעָדָה]?

ay-FOH [kron ha-mees-a-DAH]?

246. —— the baggage car.

קְרוֹן הַמִּטְעָן.

kron ha-meet-AN.

247. —— the smoking car.

קְרוֹן הֶעָשׁוֹן.

kron ha-ee-SHOON.

248. —— the sleeper.

קְרוֹן הַשֵּׁנָה.

kron ha-shay-NAH.

249. May I smoke?

הֲמֻתָּר לִי לְעַשֵּׁן?

ha-moo-TAHR lee luh-a-SHAYN?

250. Is this seat taken?

הַאִם מָקוֹם זֶה תָּפוּס?

ha-EEM ma-KOM zeh ta-FOOS?

BUS

אוטובוס

251. What bus do I take to ——?

אֵיזֶה אוֹטוֹבּוּס עָלַי לָקַחַת לְ——?

AY-zeh o-to-BOOS a-LIE la-KA-khat luh——?

252. How much is the fare?

כַּמָּה עוֹלָה הַנְּסִיעָה?

ka-MAH o-LAH han-see-AH?

253. Where does the bus for —— stop?

אֵיפֹה עוֹמֵד הָאוֹטוֹבּוּס לְ——?

ay-FOH o-MED ha-o-to-BOOS luh——?

254. Driver. do you go near ——?

נֶהָג, הַאִם אַתָּה עוֹבֵר עַל יַד ——?

neh-HAG. ha-EEM a-TAH o-VAYR al yad ——?

255. Will I have to change?

הַאִם עָלַי לְהַחֲלִיף?

ha-EEM a-LIE luh-ha-kha-LEEF?

256. Please tell me where to get off.

נָא לוֹמַר לִי אֵיפֹה עָלַי לָרֶדֶת.

nah lo-MAHR lee ay-FOH a-LIE la-REH-det.

257. I want to get off at the next stop.

אֲבַקֵשׁ לָרֶדֶת בַּתַּחֲנָה הַבָּאָה.

a-va-KAYSH la-REH-det ba-ta-kha-NAH ha-ba-AH.

TAXI

טַקְסִי

258. Please call a taxi for me.

אֲבַקֵשׁ לִקְרֹא לְטַקְסִי   עֲבוּרִי.

a-va-KAYSH leek-RO luh-TAK-see a-voo-REE.

259. Are you free?

(הַאִם אַתָּה) חָפְשִׁי?

(ha-EEM a-TAH, то м.) *khof-SHEE?*

260. What is the price [per hour] per kilometer?

מַה הַמְּחִיר [לְשָׁעָה] לְקִילוֹמֶטֶר?

MAH ha-muh-KHEER [luh-sha-AH] luh-kee-lo-MEH-tehr?

261. How much will the ride cost?

כַּמָּה תַּעֲלֶה הַנְּסִיעָה?

ka-MAH ta-a-LEH han-see-AH?

262. I would like to drive through the city for an hour.

בִּרְצוֹנִי לִנְסֹעַ דֶּרֶךְ הָעִיר לְשָׁעָה.

beer-tso-NEE leen-SO-a DEH-rekh ha-EER luh-sha-AH.

263. Drive more slowly, please.

(סַע) יוֹתֵר לְאַט בְּבַקָּשָׁה.

(sa, TO M.) yo-TAYR luh-AT buh-va-ka-SHAH.

264. Can you stop here?

(הֲתוּכַל) לַעֲמֹד פֹּה?

(ha-too-KHAL, TO M.) la-a-MOD poh?

265. Wait for me, please.

(חַכֵּה לִי), בְּבַקָּשָׁה.

(kha-KAY lee, TO M.) buh-va-ka-SHAH.

AUTOMOBILE TRAVEL

סִיּוּר בַּמְּכוֹנִית.

266. Where can I rent [a car]?

אֵיפֹה אוּכַל לִשְׂכֹּר [מְכוֹנִית]?

ay-FOH oo-KHAL lees-KOR [muh-kho-NEET]?

267. —— a motorcycle.

אוֹפַנוֹעַ.

off-NOH-a.

268. I have an international driver's license.

יֵשׁ לִי רִשְׁיוֹן נֵהָגוּת בֵּינְלְאוּמִי.

yesh lee reesh-YON neh-ha-GOOT bayn-luh-oo-MEE.

269. What [town] is this?

אֵיזוֹ [עִיר] זֹאת?

AY-zo [EER] zot?

270. —— settlement.

מוֹשָׁבָה.

mo-sha-VAH.

271. What suburb is [this]?

אֵיזֶה פַּרְוָר[זֶה]?

AY-zeh par-VAHR [zeh]?

272. —— the next one.

הַבָּא.

ha-BAH.

273. Where does that road go?

לְאָן מוֹבִיל כְּבִישׁ זֶה?

luh-AN mo-VEEL kveesh zeh?

274. Is the road [rough]?

הַאִם הַכְּבִישׁ [קָשֶׁה]?

ha-EEM hak-VEESH [ka-SHEH]?

275. —— smooth.

חָלָק.

kha-LAK.

276. —— paved.

סָלוּל.

sa-LOOL.

277. —— bad.

רַע.

rah.

278. ——— good.

טוב.

tov.

279. Can you show it to me on the road map?

(הַתּוּכַל) (הַתּוּכְלִי) לְהַרְאוֹת לִי אוֹתוֹ עַל הַמַּפָּה?

(ha-too-KHAL, TO M.) (ha-tookh-LEE, TO F.) luh-har-OT lee o-TOH al ha-ma-PAH?

280. Where can I find [a gas station] a garage?

אֵיפֹה אֶמְצָא [תַּחֲנַת דֶּלֶק] מוּסָךְ?

ay-FOH em-TSAH [ta-kha-NAT DEH-lek] moo-SAKH?

281. The tank is [empty] full.

הַטַּנְק [רֵיק] מָלֵא.

ha-TANK [rayk] ma-LAY.

282. How much does a liter of gas cost?

כַּמָּה עוֹלֶה לִיטֶר בֶּנְזִין?

ka-MAH o-LEH LEE-tehr ben-ZEEN?

283. Give me forty liters.

(תֵּן) לִי אַרְבָּעִים לִיטֶר.

(tayn, TO M.) lee ar-ba-EEM LEE-tehr.

284. Change the oil, please.

(הַחֲלֵף) אֶת הַשֶּׁמֶן, בְּבַקָּשָׁה.

(ha kha-LEF, TO M.) et ha-SHEH-men, buh-va-ka-SHAH.

285. [Light] oil.

שֶׁמֶן [קַל]

SHEH-men [kal].

286. Put water in the battery.

(שִׂים) מַיִם בַּסוֹלְלָה.

(seem, TO M.) MAH-yeem ba-soh-luh-LAH.

287. Charge the battery.

(הַטְעֵן) אֶת הַסוֹלְלָה.

(hat-AYN, TO M.) *et ha-so-luh-LAH.*

288. Lubricate the car.

(שַׁמֵּן) אֶת הַמְכוֹנִית.

(sha-MAYN, TO M.) *et ha-muh-kho-NEET.*

289. Clean the windshield.

(נַקֵּה) אֶת הַשִּׁמְשָׁה.

(na-KAY, TO M.) *et ha-sheem-SHAH.*

290. Could you wash it soon?

(הֲתוּכַל) לִרְחוֹץ אוֹתָהּ עוֹד מְעַט?

(ha-too-KHAL, TO M.) *leer-KHOTS o-TAH od muh-AT?*

291. I wish to leave my car here for the night.

בִּרְצוֹנִי לְהַשְׁאִיר אֶת הַמְכוֹנִית שֶׁלִּי פֹּה לַלַּיְלָה.

beer-TSO-nee luh-hash-EER et ha-muh-kho-NEET sheh-LEE poh la-LIE-lah.

292. Can you recommend a good mechanic?

הַאִם (תּוּכַל) (תּוּכְלִי) לְהַמְלִיץ עַל מְכוֹנַאי טוֹב?

ha-EEM (too-KHAL; TO M.) *(tookh-LEE,* TO F.) *luh-ham-LEETS al muh-kho-nah-EE tov?*

293. Adjust the brakes.

(הַתְאֵם) אֶת הַמַּעֲצוֹרִים.

(hat-AYM, TO M.) *et ha-ma-a-tso-REEM.*

294. Check the tires.

(בְּדֹק) אֶת הַצְּמִיגִים.

(buh-DOHK, TO M.) *et ha-tsmee-GEEM.*

295. Can you repair a flat tire?

(הֲתוּכַל) לְתַקֵּן פַּנְטְשֶׁר?

(ha-too-KHAL, to m.) luh-ta-KAYN pant-SHEHR?

296. The car does not move.

הַמְּכוֹנִית לֹא זָזָה.

ha-muh-kho-NEET loh ZA-za.

297. The motor overheats.

הַמּוֹטוֹר מִתְחַמֵּם יוֹתֵר מִדַּי.

ha-moh-TOR meet-kha-MEM yo-TAYR mee-DIE.

298. There is [a grinding noise].

יֵשׁ [רַעַשׁ טְחִינָה].

yesh [RAH-ash tuh-khee-NAH].

299. —— a rattling noise.

רַעַשׁ דְּפִיקָה.

RAH-ash duh-fee-KAH.

300. —— a slow leak.

דֶּלֶף אִטִּי.

DEH-lef ee-TEE.

301. May I park here for a few hours?

הַאוּכַל לַחֲנוֹת פֹּה לְכַמָּה שָׁעוֹת?

ha-oo-KHAL la-kha-NOT poh leh-kha-MAH shah-OT?

HELP ON THE ROAD

עֶזְרָה בַּדֶּרֶךְ

302. I am sorry to trouble you.

אֲנִי (מִצְטַעֵר) לְהַטְרִיחַ (אוֹתָךְ).

a-NEE (meets-ta-AYR, m.) luh-hat-REE-akh (o-TAKH, to f.).

303. I am sorry to trouble you.

אֲנִי (מִצְטַעֶרֶת) לְהַטְרִיחַ (אוֹתְךָ).

a-NEE (meets-ta-EH-ret, F.) luh-hat-REE-akh (ot-
KHAH, TO M.).

304. My car has broken down.

הַמְּכוֹנִית שֶׁלִּי הִתְקַלְקְלָה.

ha-muh-kho-NEET sheh-LEE heet-kal-kuh-LAH.

305. Will you help me get it to the side of the road?

(הֲתוּכַל) לַעֲזוֹר לִי לְהַעֲבִיר אוֹתָהּ לְצַד הַכְּבִישׁ?

(ha-too-KHAL, TO M.) la-a-ZOR lee luh-ha-a-VEER
o-TAH luh-TSAD hak-VEESH?

306. Can you push the car?

(הֲתוּכַל) לִדְחוֹף אֶת הַמְּכוֹנִית?

(ha-too-KHAL, TO M.) leed-KHOF et ha-muh-kho-
NEET?

307. Can you help me change a tire?

(הֲתוּכַל) לַעֲזוֹר לִי לְהַחֲלִיף צָמִיג

(ha-too-KHAL, TO M.) la-a-ZOR lee luh-ha-kha-
LEEF tsa-MEEG?

308. Can you lend me a jack?

(הֲתוּכַל) לְהַשְׁאִיל לִי מַנְיֵף?

(ha-too-KHAL, TO M.) luh-hash-EEL lee may-
NEEF?

309. My car is stuck [in the mud] in the ditch.

הַמְּכוֹנִית שֶׁלִּי נִתְקְעָה [בַּבּוֹץ] בַּתְּעָלָה.

ha-muh-kho-NEET sheh-LEE neet-kuh-AH [ba-
BOTS] ba-tuh-a-LAH.

310. Could you take me to a garage?

(הֲתוּכַל) לָקַחַת אוֹתִי לְמוּסָךְ?

(*ha-too-KHAL*, TO M.) *la-KA-khat o-TEE luh-moo-SAKH?*

PARTS OF THE CAR

חֶלְקֵי הַמְּכוֹנִית

311. The accelerator.

הַמַּמְהִיר.

ha-mam-HEER.

312. The battery.

הַסוֹלְלָה.

ha-soh-luh-LAH.

313. The bolt.

הַבּוֹרֶג.

ha-BO-reg.

314. The brake.

הַמַּעֲצוֹר.

ha-ma-a-TSOR.

315. Clutch.

קָלְטָשׁ.

klatsh.

316. The engine.

הַמָּנוֹעַ.

ha-mah-NOH-a.

317. The gear shift.

הַחְלָפַת הַמַּהֲלָךְ.

hakh-lah-FAT ha-ma-ha-LAKH.

318. The headlight.

הָאוֹר הַקִּדְמִי.

ha-OR ha-keed-MEE.

319. The horn.

הַצּוֹפָר.

ha-tsoh-FAHR.

320. The nut.

הָאֹם.

ha-OM.

321. The spark plug.

מְגוּפַת הַזִּיקִים.

muh-goo-FAT ha-zee-KEEM.

322. The spring.

הַקְּפִיץ.

ha-kuh-FEETS.

323. The starter.

הַמַּתְנֵעַ.

ha-mat-NAY-a.

324. The steering wheel.

הַהֶגֶה.

ha-HEH-geh.

325. The tail light.

הָאוֹר הָאֲחוֹרִי.

ha-OR ha-a-kho-REE.

326. The tire.

הַצְּמִיג.

ha-tsa-MEEG.

327. The spare tire.

צְמִיג הַמִּלּוּאִים.

tsmeeg ha-mee-loo-EEM.

328. The wheel.

הָאוֹפָן.

ha-o-FAN.

329. The windshield wiper.

מְנַגֵּב הַשִּׁמְשָׁה.

muh-na-GAYV ha-sheem-SHAH.

TOOLS AND EQUIPMENT

מַכְשִׁירִים וְכֵלִים

330. The chain.

הַשַּׁלְשֶׁלֶת.

ha-shal-SHEH-let.

331. The hammer.

הַפַּטִּישׁ.

ha-pa-TEESH.

332. The jack.

הַמָּנִיף.

ha-may-NEEF.

333. The pliers.

הַצְּבָת.

ha-TSVAT.

334. The rope.

הַחֶבֶל.

ha-KHEH-vel.

335. The screwdriver.

הַמַּבְרֵג.

ha-mav-RAYG.

336. The tire pump.

מַשְׁאֵבַת הָאֲוִיר.

mash-ay-VAT ha-a-VEER.

337. The wrench.

הַמַּפְתֵּחַ.

ha-maf-TAY-akh.

ROAD SIGNS

שְׁלָטִים בַּדֶּרֶךְ

338. No thoroughfare.

אֵין מַעֲבָר.

ayn ma-ah-VAHR.

339. No parking.

אֵין חֲנָיָה.

ayn kha-nee-YAH.

340. Hospital.

בֵּית חוֹלִים.

bayt kho-LEEM.

341. School.

בֵּית סֵפֶר.

bayt SAY-fehr.

342. Detour.

דֶּרֶךְ עֲקִיפִין.

DEH-rekh a-kee-FEEN.

343. Slow down.

סַע לְאַט.

sah luh-AT.

344. Go.

סַע *or* הָלוֹךְ.

sa or ha-LOKH.

345. Road intersections *or* crossroads.

הִצְטַלְבוּת דְּרָכִים.

heets-tal-VOOT dra-KHEEM.

346. Parking.

חֲנִיָּה.

kha-nee-YAH.

347. Winding road.

כְּבִישׁ מִתְפַּתֵּל.

kveesh meet-pa-TAYL.

348. Narrow road.

כְּבִישׁ צַר.

kveesh tsahr.

349. One-way.

כִּוּוּן אֶחָד.

kee-VOON eh-KHAHD.

350. No passing.

לֹא לַעֲבוֹר.

loh la-a-VOR.

351. Steep grade.

מִדְרוֹן.

meed-RON.

352. Dip.

מוֹרָד.

mo-RAD.

353. Maximum speed —— kilometers.

מְהִירוּת מַקְסִימָלִית —— קִילוֹמֶטֶר.

muh-hee-ROOT mak-see-MAH-leet —— kee-lo-MEH-tehr.

354. Drive carefully.

סַע בִּזְהִירוּת.

sa beez-hee-ROOT.

355. Use second gear.

סַע בְּמַהֲלָךְ שֵׁנִי.

sa buh-ma-ha-LAKH shay-NEE.

356. Keep [right] left.

סַע בְּצַד [יָמִין] שְׂמֹאל.

sa buh-TSAD [yuh-MEEN] smol.

357. Curve.

סִבּוּב.

see-BOOV.

358. Double curve.

סִבּוּב כָּפוּל.

see-BOOV ka-FOOL.

359. Sharp turn.

סִבּוּב חַד.

see-BOOV khad.

360. Stop.

עֲצוֹר.

a-TSOR.

361. Stop, border.

עֲצוֹר, גְּבוּל.

a-TSOR, gvool.

362. No [right] left turn.

פְּנִיָה [יְמָנִית] שְׂמָאלִית אֲסוּרָה.

puh-nee-YAH [yuh-ma-NEET] smo-LEET a-soo-RAH.

363. Railroad crossing.

פַּסֵּי רַכֶּבֶת.

pa-SAY ra-KEH-vet.

364. Road repairs.

תִּקּוּנִים בַּכְּבִישׁ.

tee-koo-NEEM bak-VEESH.

PUBLIC NOTICES

מוֹדָעוֹת צִבּוּרִיּוֹת

365. No admittance.

אֵין כְּנִיסָה.

ayn kuh-nee-SAH.

366. No trespassing.

אֵין מַעֲבָר.

ayn ma-a-VAHR.

367. Push.

דְּחוֹף.

duh-KHOF.

368. The public is requested to ———.

הַקָּהָל מִתְבַּקֵּשׁ לְ———.

ha-ka-HAL meet-ba-KAYSH luh———.

369. Vacant.

פָּנוּי.

pah-NOOY.

370. Exit.

יְצִיאָה.

yuh-tsee-AH.

371. Entrance.

כְּנִיסָה.

kuh-nee-SAH.

372. Come in.

הִכָּנֵס, *or* יָבוֹא.

hee-ka-NAYS or ya-VOH.

373. No spitting.

לֹא לִירוֹק.

loh lee-ROK.

374. No smoking.

לֹא לְעַשֵּׁן.

loh luh-a-SHAYN.

375. Pull.

מְשׁוֹךְ.

muh-SHOKH.

376. Push.

דְּחוֹף.

duh-KHOF.

377. Closed.

סָגוּר.

sa-GOOR.

378. Open.

פָּתוּחַ.

pa-TOO-akh.

379. Danger.

סַכָּנָה.

sa-ka-NAH.

380. Ring.

צַלְצֵל.

tsal-TSAYL.

381. For rent.

לְהַשְׂכִּיר.

luh-has-KEER.

COMMUNICATIONS: TELEPHONE

תַּחְבּוּרָה: טֶלֶפוֹן

382. May I telephone from here?

הַאוּכַל לְטַלְפֵּן מִפֹּה?

ha-oo-KHAL luh-tal-PAYN mee-POH?

383. Will you telephone for me?

(הֲתוּכַל) (הֲתוּכְלִי) לְטַלְפֵּן עֲבוּרִי?

(ha-too-KHAL, TO M.) (ha-tookh-LEE, TO F.) luh-tal-PAYN a-voo-REE?

384. I want to make a local call, number ——.

אֲבַקֵּשׁ שִׂיחָה מְקוֹמִית, מִסְפָּר ——.

a-va-KAYSH see-KHAH muh-ko-MEET, mees-PAHR ——.

385. My number is ———.

מִסְפָּרִי הוּא ———.

mees-pah-REE hoo ———.

386. How much is a long-distance call to ———?

כַּמָּה עוֹלָה שִׂיחַת חוּץ לְ———?

ka-MAH o-LAH see-KHAT khoots luh———?

387. The operator will call you.

פְּקִידַת הַטֶּלֶפוֹן תִּקְרָא (לְךָ) (לָךְ).

puh-kee-DAT ha-teh-leh-FON teek-RAH (luh-KHAH
   TO M.) *(lakh,* TO F.).

388. Hello, hello.

הַלוֹ, הַלוֹ.

ha-LOH, ha-LOH.

389. They do not answer.

הֵם אֵינָם עוֹנִים.

haym ay-NAM o-NEEM.

390. The line is busy.

הַמִּסְפָּר תָּפוּס.

ha-mees-PAHR ta-FOOS.

391. This is Mr. ——— speaking.

פֹּה מְדַבֵּר מַר ———.

poh muh-da-BAYR mahr ———.

392. Please hold the line.

אֲבַקֵּשׁ לְחַכּוֹת רֶגַע.

a-va-KAYSH luh-kha-KOT REH-ga.

393. He is not at home.

הוּא אֵינוֹ בַּבַּיִת.

hoo ay-NO ba-BAH-yeet.

394. Can I leave a message?

הַאוּכַל לִמְסֹר מַשֶּׁהוּ?

ha-oo-KHAL lim-SOHR mah-sheh-HOO?

395. I will call back later.

אֲצַלְצֵל עוֹד פַּעַם יוֹתֵר מְאוּחָר.

a-tsal-TSAYL od PAH-am yo-TAYR muh-oo-KHAHR.

396. There is a telephone call for you.

יֵשׁ שִׂיחַת טֶלֶפוֹן (בִּשְׁבִילְךָ) (בִּשְׁבִילֵךְ).

yesh see-KHAT teh-leh-FON (beesh-veel-KHAH, TO
M.*) (beesh-vee-LAYKH,* TO F.*).*

POST OFFICE

מִשְׂרַד הַדֹּאַר

397. I am looking for the post office.

אֲנִי (מְחַפֵּשׂ) (מְחַפֶּשֶׂת) אֶת מִשְׂרַד הַדֹּאַר.

a-NEE (muh kha-PAYS, M.*) (muh-kha-PEH-set,* F.*)
et mees-RAD ha-DO-ar.*

398. A letter box.

תֵּיבַת דֹּאַר.

tay-VAT DO-ar.

399. To which window should I go?

לְאֵיזֶה אֶשְׁנָב עָלַי לָגֶשֶׁת?

luh-AY-zeh esh-NAV a-LIE la-GEH-shet?

400. I want to send this [via airmail].

בִּרְצוֹנִי לִשְׁלֹחַ זֹאת [בְּדֹאַר אֲוִיר].

beer-tso-NEE leesh-LO-akh zot [buh-DO-ar a-VEER].

401. —— regular mail.

דֹּאַר רָגִיל.

DO-ar ra-GEEL.

402. —— registered mail.

דֹּאַר רָשׁוּם.

DO-ar ra-SHOOM.

403. —— parcel post.

דֹּאַר חֲבִילוֹת.

DO-ar kha-vee-LOT.

404. —— special delivery.

דֹּאַר אֶקְסְפְּרֶס.

DO-ar eks-PRES.

405. —— air freight.

מִטְעָן אֲוִיר.

meet-AN a-VEER.

406. I would like to insure this package for ——.

בִּרְצוֹנִי לְבַטֵּחַ חֲבִילָה זוֹ עֲבוּר ——.

beer-tso-NEE luh-va-TAY-akh kha-vee-LAH zoo a-VOOR ——.

407. Please give me [six stamps].

אֲבַקֵשׁ [שִׁשָּׁה בּוּלִים].

a-va-KAYSH [shee-SHAH boo-LEEM].

408. Will it go out today?

הַאִם זֶה יֵצֵא הַיּוֹם?

ha-EEM zeh yay-TSAY ha-YOM?

409. I want to send a money order.

בִּרְצוֹנִי לִשְׁלוֹחַ הַמְחָאַת כֶּסֶף.

beer-tso-NEE leesh-LO-akh ham-kha-AT KEH-sef.

TELEGRAM : CABLEGRAM

מִבְרָק: וְאֵלְחוּט

410. I wish to send [a telegram or cablegram].

בִּרְצוֹנִי לִשְׁלוֹחַ [מִבְרָק].

beer-tso-NEE leesh-LO-akh [meev-RAK].

411. —— a night letter.

מִבְרָק לַיְלָה.

meev-RAK LIE-lah.

412. What is the word rate to New York?

כַּמָּה עוֹלָה הַמִּלָּה לְנִיוּ יוֹרְק?

ka-MAH o-LAH ha-mee-LAH luh-"New York"?

413. I will pay for the reply.

אֲשַׁלֵּם עֲבוּר הַתְּשׁוּבָה.

a-sha-LAYM a-VOOR ha-tuh-shoo-VAH.

414. When will it arrive?

מָתַי זֶה יַגִּיעַ?

ma-TIE zeh ya-GEE-a?

HOTEL

מָלוֹן

415. I am looking for a good hotel.

אֲנִי (מְחַפֵּשׂ) (מְחַפֶּשֶׂת) מָלוֹן טוֹב.

a-NEE (muh-kha-PAYS, M.) (muh-kha-PEH-set, F.)
ma-LON tov.

416. The best hotel.

הַמָּלוֹן הַטּוֹב בְּיוֹתֵר.

ha-ma-LON ha-TOV buh-yo-TAYR.

417. An inexpensive hotel.

מָלוֹן לֹא יָקָר.

ma-LON loh ya-KAHR.

418. A boarding house.

פֶּנְסִיוֹן.

pen-SYON.

419. I want to be in the center of town.

אֲנִי (רוֹצֶה) (רוֹצָה) לִהְיוֹת בְּמֶרְכַּז הָעִיר.

a-NEE (ro-TSEH, M.) (ro-TSAH, F.) luh-hee-YOT buh-mehr-KAZ ha-EER.

420. Where it is not noisy.

אֵיפֹה שֶׁאֵין רַעַשׁ.

ay-FOH shuh-AYN RAH-ash.

421. I have a reservation for today.

הִזְמַנְתִּי חֶדֶר לְהַיּוֹם.

heez-MAN-tee KHEH-dehr luh-ha-YOM.

422. Do you have [a room]?

יֵשׁ לָכֶם [חֶדֶר]?

yesh la-khem [KHEH-dehr]?

423. —— a single room.

חֶדֶר יָחִיד.

KHEH-dehr ya-KHEED.

424. —— a double room.

חֶדֶר כָּפוּל.

KHEH-dehr ka-FOOL.

425. —— a room with air conditioning.

חֶדֶר עִם קֵרוּר אֲוִיר.

KHEH-dehr eem kay-ROOR a-VEER.

426. —— a suite.

מַעֲרֶכֶת חֲדָרִים.

ma-a-REH-khet kha-da-REEM.

427. I want a room [with a double bed].

אֲבַקֵּשׁ חֶדֶר [עִם מִטָּה כְּפוּלָה].

a-va-KAYSH KHEH-dehr [eem mee-TAH kuh-foo-LAH].

428. —— with twin beds.

עִם שְׁתֵּי מִטּוֹת.

eem shtay mee-TOT.

429. —— with a bath.

עִם אַמְבַּטְיָה.

eem am-BAT-yah.

430. —— with a shower.

עִם מִקְלַחַת.

eem meek-LAH-khat.

431. —— with hot water.

עִם מַיִם חַמִּים.

eem MAH-yeem kha-MEEM.

432. —— with a balcony.

עִם מִרְפֶּסֶת.

eem meer-PEH-set.

433. I will take a room [for tonight].

אֶקַּח חֶדֶר [לְהַלַּיְלָה].

e-KAKH KHEH-dehr [luh-ha-LIE-lah].

434. —— for several days.

לְכַמָּה יָמִים.

luh-kha-MAH ya-MEEM.

435. —— for two persons.

לִשְׁנֵי אֲנָשִׁים.

leesh-NAY a-na-SHEEM.

436. May I have it [with] without meals?

הַאוּכַל לְקַבֵּל אוֹתוֹ [עִם] בְּלִי אֲרוּחוֹת?

ha-oo-KHAL luh-ka-BAYL o-TOH [eem] buh-LEE a-roo-KHOT?

437. What is the rate per day?

מַה הַמְּחִיר לְיוֹם?

mah ha-muh-KHEER luh-YOM?

438. Are tax and service included?

הַאִם זֶה כּוֹלֵל מִסִים וְשֵׁרוּת?

ha-EEM zeh ko-LAYL mee-SEEM vuh-shay-ROOT?

439. I would like to see the room.

אֲבַקֵשׁ לִרְאוֹת אֶת הַחֶדֶר.

a-va-KAYSH leer-OT et ha-KHEH-dehr.

440. I do not like this one.

זֶה לֹא מוֹצֵא חֵן בְּעֵינַי.

zeh loh mo-TSAY khen buh-ay-NIE.

441. Have you something [better]?

הֲיֵשׁ לָכֶם מַשֶּׁהוּ [יוֹתֵר טוֹב]?

ha-yesh la-khem MAH-shuh-hoo [yo-TAYR tov]?

442. —— cheaper.

יוֹתֵר זוֹל.

yo-TAYR zol.

443. —— larger.

יוֹתֵר גָּדוֹל.

yo-TAYR ga-DOL.

444. —— smaller.

יוֹתֵר קָטָן.

yo-TAYR ka-TAN.

445. A [front room] back room.

[חֶדֶר קִדְמִי] חֶדֶר אֲחוֹרִי.

[KHEH-dehr keed-MEE] KHEH-dehr a-kho-REE.

446. On a [lower floor] higher floor.

עַל [קוֹמָה יוֹתֵר נְמוּכָה] קוֹמָה יוֹתֵר עֶלְיוֹנָה.

al [ko-MAH yo-TAYR nuh-moo-KHAH] ko-MAH yo-TAYR el-yo-NAH.

447. With more [light] air.

עִם יוֹתֵר [אוֹר] אֲוִיר.

eem yo-TAYR [or] a-VEER.

448. Upstairs.

לְמַעְלָה.

luh-MAH-a-lah.

449. Downstairs.

לְמַטָּה.

luh-MAH-tah.

450. Is there an elevator?

הַאִם יֵשׁ מַעֲלִית?

ha-EEM yesh mah-a-LEET?

451. What is my room number?

מַה מִסְפַּר חַדְרִי?

mah mees-PAHR khed-REE?

452. Please sign the hotel register.

נָא לַחְתּוֹם עַל רְשִׁימַת הָאוֹרְחִים.

nah lakh-TOM al ruh-shee-MAT ha-or-KHEEM.

453. My room key, please.

מַפְתֵּחַ חַדְרִי, בְּבַקָּשָׁה.

maf-TAY-akh khed-REE, buh-va-ka-SHAH.

454. Please send [the chambermaid].

אֲבַקֵּשׁ לִשְׁלוֹחַ [אֶת הַמְשָׁרֶתֶת].

a-va-KAYSH leesh-LO-akh [et ha-muh-sha-REH-tet].

455. —— a waiter.

מֶלְצָר.

mel-TSAHR.

456. —— a porter.

סַבָּל.

sa-BAL.

457. —— a messenger *or* valet.

שָׁלִיחַ.

sha-LEE-akh.

458. Who is it?

מִי זֶה?

mee zeh?

459. Please [call me] wake me at 9 o'clock.

אֲבַקֵּשׁ [לִקְרֹא לִי] לְהָעִיר אוֹתִי בְּשָׁעָה תֵּשַׁע.

a-va-KAYSH [leek-ROH lee] luh-ha-EER o-TEE buh-sha-AH TAY-sha.

460. I would like to have breakfast in my room.

אֲבַקֵּשׁ אֲרוּחַת בֹּקֶר בְּחַדְרִי.

a-va-KAYSH a-roo-KHAT BO-kehr buh-khad-REE.

461. I want to speak to the manager.

אֲבַקֵּשׁ לְדַבֵּר עִם הַמְנַהֵל.

a-va-KAYSH luh-da-BAYR eem ha-muh-na-HAYL.

462. I am looking for [a nurse].

אֲנִי מְחַפֵּשׂ [אָחוֹת].

a-.NEE muh-kha-PAYS [ah-KHOHT].

463. —— baby sitter.

מְטַפֶּלֶת.

muh-ta-PEH-let.

464. Are there any letters or messages for me?

הַאִם יֵשׁ אֵיזֶה מִכְתָּבִים אוֹ יְדִיעוֹת בִּשְׁבִילִי?

ha-EEM yaysh AY-zeh meekh-ta-VEEM o yuh-dee-OT beesh-vee-LEE?

465. I am expecting a visitor.

אֲנִי (מְחַכֶּה) (מְחַכָּה) לְאוֹרֵחַ.

a-NEE (muh kha-KEH, м.) (muh-kha-KAH, F.) luh-o-RAY-akh.

466. —— a telephone call.

שִׂיחָה טֶלֶפוֹנִית.

see-KHAH teh-leh-FO-neet.

467. —— a package.

חֲבִילָה.

kha-vee-LAH.

468. When do I have to check out?

בְּאֵיזֶה שָׁעָה עָלַי לָצֵאת?

buh-AY-zeh sha-AH a-LIE la-TSAYT?

469. I would like my bill now because I am leaving immediately.

אֲבַקֵּשׁ אֶת הַחֶשְׁבּוֹן שֶׁלִּי עַכְשָׁו כִּי אֲנִי (יוֹצֵא)
(יוֹצֵאת) תֵּכֶף.

a-va-KAYSH et ha-khesh-BON sheh-LEE akh-SHAHV kee a-NEE (yo-TSAY, м.) (yo-TSAYT, ғ.) TAY-khef.

470. Can I give you a check?

הַאוּכַל לָתֵת לָכֶם צֶ׳קּ?

ha-oo-KHAL la-TAYT la-khem "check"?

471. Forward [my mail] to American Express at Paris.

תִּשְׁלְחוּ [אֶת הַדֹּאַר שֶׁלִּי] לְאַמֶרִיקַן אֶקְסְפְּרֶס
בְּפָּרִיס.

teesh-luh-KHOO [et ha-DO-ar sheh-LEE] luh-a-MEH-ree-kan eks-PRES buh-pa-REES.

CHAMBERMAID

מְשָׁרֶתֶת

472. Do not disturb me until 7 o'clock.

נָא לֹא לְהַפְרִיעַ לִי עַד שָׁעָה שֶׁבַע.

nah loh luh-haf-REE-a lee ad sha-AH SHEH-va.

473. [The door] the lock does not work well.

[הַדֶּלֶת] הַמַּנְעוּל לֹא בְּסֵדֶר.

[ha-DEH-let] ha-man-OOL loh buh-SAY-dehr.

474. It is too [cold] hot in the room.

יוֹתֵר מִדַּי [קַר] חַם בַּחֶדֶר.

yo-TAYR mee-DIE [kahr] kham ba-KHEH-dehr.

475. Could I have some laundry done?

הַאוּכַל לָתֵת כַּמָּה דְּבָרִים לְכַבֵּס?

ha-oo-KHAL la-TAYT ka-MAH duh-va-REEM luh-kha-BAYS?

476. Bring me another blanket, please.

(הָבִיאִי) לִי עוֹד שְׂמִיכָה, בְּבַקָּשָׁה.

(ha-VEE-ee, TO F.*) lee od smee-KHAH, buh-va-ka-SHAH.*

477. A bath mat.

שָׁטִיחַ אַמְבַּטְיָה.

shuh-TEE-akh am-BAT-yah.

478. Some coat hangers.

קוֹלָבִים אֲחָדִים.

ko-lah-VEEM a-khah-DEEM.

479. A glass.

כּוֹס.

kos.

480. A pillow.

כַּר.

kahr.

481. A pillow case.

צִפִּיָּה.

tsee-pee-YAH.

482. Soap.

סַבּוֹן.

sa-BON.

483. Toilet paper.

נְיָר בֵּית כִּסֵּא.

nee-YAHR bayt kee-SAY.

484. Some towels.

כַּמָּה מַגָּבוֹת.

ka-MAH ma-ga-VOT.

485. Some washcloths.

כַּמָּה מַטְלִיּוֹת.

ka-MAH mat-lee-YOT.

486. Please change the sheets.

אֲבַקֵּשׁ לְהַחֲלִיף אֶת הַסְּדִינִים.

a-va-KAYSH luh-ha-kha-LEEF et has-dee-NEEM.

487. Make up my bed.

(סַדְּרִי) אֶת מִטָּתִי.

(sad-REE, TO F.) *et mee-ta-TEE.*

488. Come back later, please.

(שׁוּבִי) אַחַר כָּךְ, בְּבַקָּשָׁה.

(SHOO-vee, TO F.) *a-KHAHR kakh, buh-va-ka-SHAH.*

APARTMENT

דִּירָה

489. I am looking for a furnished apartment.

אֲנִי (מְחַפֵּשׂ) (מְחַפֶּשֶׂת) דִּירָה מְרוּהֶטֶת.

a-NEE (muh kha-PAYS, M.) *(muh-kha-PEH-set,* F.) *dee-RAH muh-roo-HEH-tet.*

490. With a bathroom.

עִם אַמְבַּטְיָה.

eem am-BAT-yah.

491. With a shower.

עִם מִקְלַחַת.

eem meek-LA-khat.

492. With a dining room.

עִם חֲדַר אֹכֶל.

eem kha-DAHR O-khel.

493. With a kitchen.

עִם מִטְבָּח.

eem meet-BAKH.

494. With a living room.

עִם סָלוֹן.

eem sa-LON.

495. Do you furnish the linen?

(הַאִם אַתְּ נוֹתֶנֶת) אֶת הַסְּדִינִים?

(ha-EEM at no-TEH-net, TO F.) et has-dee-NEEM?

496. The dishes.

הַצַּלָּחוֹת.

ha-tsa-la-la-KHOT.

497. The cooking utensils.

כְּלֵי הַבִּשּׁוּל.

kluy ha-bee-SHOOL.

498. Do you know a good cook?

(הַאִם אַתְּ יוֹדַעַת) עַל מְבַשֶּׁלֶת טוֹבָה?

(ha-EEM at yo-DAH-at, TO F.) al muh-va-SHEH-let to-VAH?

499. A housemaid.

עוֹזֶרֶת.

o-ZEH-ret.

CAFÉ

בֵּית קָפֶה

500. Bartender, I'd like to have [a drink].

מֶלְצָר, אֲבַקֵּשׁ [מַשְׁקֶה].

mel-TSAHR, a-va-KAYSH [mash-KEH].

501. —— a cocktail.

קוֹקְטֵיל.

KOK-tayl.

502. —— a fruit drink.

מִיץ פֵּירוֹת.

meets pay-ROT.

503. —— a [small] large bottle of mineral water.

בַּקְבּוּק סוֹדָה [קָטָן] גָּדוֹל.

bak-BOOK SO-da [ka-TAN] ga-DOL.

504. —— some [light] dark beer.

בִּירָה [בְּהִירָה] כֵּהָה.

BEE-ra [buh-hee-RAH] kay-HAH.

505. —— some champagne.

יֵין שַׁמְפַּנְיָה.

yayn sham-PAN-yah.

506. —— some cognac.

קוֹנְיָק *or* יֵין שָׂרָף.

kon-YAK or yayin sa-RAF.

507. —— a cordial *or* liqueur.

לִיקֵר.

lee-KEHR.

508. —— a glass of [port] sherry.

כּוֹס [פּוֹרְט] שֶׁרִי.

kos [port] SHEH-ree.

509. —— some [white] red wine.

יַיִן [לָבָן] אָדֹם.

YA-yeen [la-VAN] a-DOM.

510. Let's have another.

נִשְׁתֶּה עוֹד כּוֹס.

neesh-TEH od kos.

511. To your health!

לְחַיִּים!

luh-KHA-yeem !

RESTAURANT

מִסְעָדָה

512. Can you recommend a restaurant?

הַאִם (אַתָּה יָכוֹל) (אַתְּ יְכוֹלָה) לְהַמְלִיץ עַל מִסְעָדָה?

ha-EEM (a-TAH ya-KHOL, то м.) (at yuh-kho-LAH, то f.) luh-ham-LEETS al mees-a-DAH ?

513. For breakfast.

לַאֲרוּחַת בֹּקֶר.

la-a-roo-KHAT BO-kehr.

514. For lunch.

לַאֲרוּחַת צָהֳרַיִם.

la-a-roo-KHAT tso-ha-RAH-yeem.

515. For supper.

לַאֲרוּחַת עֶרֶב.

la-a-roo-KHAT EH-rev.

516. For a sandwich.

לְכָרִיךְ.

luh-ka-REEKH.

517. At what time is dinner served?

בְּאֵיזוֹ שָׁעָה מַגִּישִׁים אֲרוּחַת עֶרֶב?

*buh-AY-zo sha-AH ma-gee-SHEEM a-roo-KHAT
EH-rev?*

518. Can we eat now?

הַאִם נוּכַל לֶאֱכֹל עַכְשָׁיו?

ha-EEM noo-KHAL leh-eh-KHOL akh-SHAHV?

519. Are you my waitress?

הַאִם אַתְּ הַמֶּלְצָרִית שֶׁלִּי?

ha-EEM at ha-mel-tsa-REET sheh-LEE?

520. Are you [my waiter]?

הַאִם אַתָּה [הַמֶּלְצָר שֶׁלִּי]?

ha-EEM a-TAH [ha-mel-TSAHR sheh-LEE]?

521. —— the headwaiter.

הַמֶּלְצָר הָרָאשִׁי.

ha-mel-TSAHR ha-ra-SHEE.

522. —— the wine steward.

מֶלְצַר הַיַּיְנוֹת.

mel-TSAHR ha-yay-NOT.

523. Waiter!

מֶלְצָר!

mel-TSAHR!

524. Give us a table near the window.

(תֵּן, TO M.) לָנוּ שׁוּלְחָן עַל יַד הַחַלוֹן.

(tayn, TO M.) LA-noo shool-KHAN al yad ha-kha-LON.

525. Outside.

בַּחוּץ.

ba-KHOOTS.

526. Inside.

בִּפְנִים.

beef-NEEM.

527. At the side.

בַּצַּד.

ba-TSAD.

528. In the corner.

בַּפִּנָּה.

ba-pee-NAH.

529. For four persons.

לְאַרְבָּעָה אֲנָשִׁים.

luh-ar-ba-AH a-na-SHEEM.

530. Please serve us quickly.

נָא לְהַגִּישׁ לָנוּ מַהֵר.

nah luh-ha-GEESH LA-noo ma-HAYR.

531. We want to order [à la carte] table d'hôte.

אֲנַחְנוּ רוֹצִים לְהַזְמִין [לְפִי הַתַּפְרִיט] אֶת אֲרוּחַת הַיּוֹם.

a-NAKH-noo ro-TSEEM luh-haz-MEEN [luh-FEE ha-taf-REET] et a-roo-KHAT ha-YOM.

532. What is the specialty of the house?

מַהוּ הַמַּאֲכָל הַמְיוּחָד שֶׁלָכֶם?

MAH-hoo ha-ma-a-KHAL ha-muh-yoo-KHAD sheh-la-KHEM?

533. Please bring me [the menu].

אֲבַקֵשׁ אֶת [הַתַּפְרִיט].

a-va-KAYSH et [ha-taf-REET].

534. —— the wine list.

רְשִׁימַת הַיֵּינוֹת.

ruh-shee-MAT ha-yay-NOT.

535. —— bread and butter.

לֶחֶם וְחֶמְאָה.

LEH-khem vuh-khem-AH.

536. —— a fork.

מַזְלֵג.

maz-LAYG.

537. —— a knife.

סַכִּין.

sa-KEEN.

538. —— a teaspoon.

כַּפִּית.

ka-PEET.

539. —— a large spoon.

כַּף.

kaf.

540. —— a napkin.

מַפִּית.

ma-PEET.

541. —— a plate.

צַלַחַת.

tsa-LA-khat.

542. I like simple food.

אֲנִי (אוֹהֵב) (אוֹהֶבֶת) אֹכֶל פָּשׁוּט.

a-NEE (o-HAYV, M.) (o-HEH-vet, F.) O-khel pa-SHOOT.

543. Oriental food.

אֹכֶל מִזְרָחִי.

O-khel meez-rah-KHEE.

544. Not too spicy.

לֹא מְפֻלְפָּל בְּיוֹתֵר.

loh muh-fool-PAL buh-yo-TAYR.

545. Not too sweet.

לֹא מָתוֹק בְּיוֹתֵר.

loh ma-TOK buh-yo-TAYR.

546. Not too sour.

לֹא חָמוּץ בְּיוֹתֵר.

loh kha-MOOTS buh-yo-TAYR.

547. Without too much fat.

בְּלִי הַרְבֵּה שֶׁמֶן.

buh-LEE har-BAY SHEH-men.

548. Not too tough.

לֹא קָשֶׁה בְּיוֹתֵר.

loh ka-SHEH buh-yo-TAYR.

549. A little [more] less, please.

קְצָת [יוֹתֵר] פָּחוֹת, בְּבַקָּשָׁה.

kuh-TSAT [yo-TAYR] pa-KHOT, buh-va-ka-SHAH.

550. I have had [enough] too much.

הָיָה לִי [מַסְפִּיק] יוֹתֵר מִדַּי.

ha-YAH lee [mas-PEEK] yo-TAYR mee-DIE.

551. I like the meat cooked [rare].

אֲבַקֵּשׁ אֶת הַבָּשָׂר מְבוּשָּׁל [לְמֶחֱצָה].

a-va KAYSH et ha-ba-SAR muh-voo-SHAL [luh-meh-kheh-TSAH].

552. —— medium.

בֵּינוֹנִי.

bay-no-NEE.

553. —— well done.

מְבוּשָּׁל הֵיטֵב.

muh-voo-SHAL hay-TAYV.

554. This is [overcooked] undercooked.

זֶה [מְבוּשָּׁל יוֹתֵר מִדַּי] לֹא מְבוּשָּׁל לְגַמְרֵי.

zeh [muh-voo-SHAL yo-TAYR mee-DIE] loh muh-voo-SHAL luh-GAM-ray.

555. This is cold.

זֶה קַר.

zeh kar.

556. Take it away, please.

(קַח) (קְחִי) אֶת זֶה בְּבַקָּשָׁה.

(kakh, TO M.) (kuh-KHEE, TO F.), et zeh buh-va-ka-SHAH.

557. I did not order this.

אֶת זֶה לֹא הִזְמַנְתִּי.

et zeh loh heez-MAN-tee.

558. May I change this for a salad?

הַאוּכַל לְהַחֲלִיף אֶת זֶה בְּסָלָט?

ha-oo-KHAL luh-ha-kha-LEEF et zeh buh-sa-LAT?

559. The check, please.

הַחֶשְׁבּוֹן, בְּבַקָּשָׁה.

ha-khesh-BON buh-va-ka-SHAH.

560. Is the service charge included?

הַאִם זֶה כּוֹלֵל אֶת דְּמֵי הַשֵּׁרוּת?

ha-EEM zeh ko-LEL et duh-MAY ha-shay-ROOT?

561. I think there is a mistake in the bill.

סְבוּרְנִי שֶׁיֵּשׁ שְׁגִיאָה בַּחֶשְׁבּוֹן.

suh-voo-RAH-nee sheh-YESH shuh-gee-AH ba-khesh-BON.

562. What are these charges for?

עֲבוּר מַה הַסְּכוּמִים הָאֵלֶּה?

a-VOOR mah ha-suh-khoo-MEEM ha-AY-loo?

563. The food and service were excellent.

הָאֹכֶל וְהַשֵּׁרוּת הָיוּ מְצוּיָּנִים.

ha-O-khel vuh-ha-shay-ROOT ha-YOO muh-tsoo-ya-NEEM.

564. This is for you.

זֶה (בִּשְׁבִילְךָ) (בִּשְׁבִילֵךְ).

zeh (beesh-veel-KHA, TO M.) (beesh-vee-LAYKH, TO F.).

565. Hearty appetite!

בְּתֵאָבוֹן!

buh-tay-a-VON!

FOOD LIST
רְשִׁימַת מַאֲכָלִים

566. Drinking water.
מֵי שְׁתִיָּה.
may shuh-tee-YAH.

567. Water [with] without ice.
מַיִם [עִם] בְּלִי קֶרַח.
MAH-yeem [eem] buh-LEE KEH-rakh.

568. The bread.
הַלֶּחֶם.
ha-LEH-khem.

569. Peeta—tortilla-like bread.
פִּיתָּה.
PEE-ta.

570. The butter.
הַחֶמְאָה.
ha-khem-AH.

571. The sugar.
הַסּוּכָּר.
ha-soo-KAHR.

572. The salt.
הַמֶּלַח.
ha-MEH-lakh.

573. The pepper.
הַפִּלְפֵּל.
ha-peel-PEL.

574. The sauce.
הָרוֹטֶב.
ha-RO-tev.

575. The olive oil.

שֶׁמֶן הַזַּיִת.

SHEH-*men ha-*ZAH-*yeet.*

576. The vinegar.

הַחֹמֶץ.

ha-KHO-*mets.*

577. The mustard.

הַחַרְדָּל.

ha-khar-DAL.

578. The garlic.

הַשּׁוּם.

ha-SHOOM.

579. The catsup.

הַקֶּטְשׁוּפּ.

ha-ket-SHOOP.

BREAKFAST

אֲרוּחַת בֹּקֶר

580. May I have [fruit juice].

אֲבַקֵּשׁ [מִיץ פֵּירוֹת].

a-va-KAYSH [*meets pay-*ROT].

581. —— grape juice.

מִיץ עֲנָבִים.

*meets a-na-*VEEM.

582. —— orange juice.

מִיץ תַּפּוּזִים.

*meets ta-poo-*ZEEM.

583. —— tomato juice.

מִיץ עַגְבָנִיּוֹת.

meets ag-va-nee-YOT.

584. —— stewed prunes.

שְׁזִיפִים מְבוּשָּׁלִים.

shuh-zee-FEEM muh-voo-sha-LEEM.

585. —— cooked cereal.

גְּרִיסִים *or* דַּיְסָה.

gree-SEEM or die-SAH.

586. —— toast and jam.

טוֹסְט עִם רִבָּה.

tost eem ree-BAH.

587. —— rolls.

לַחְמָנִיּוֹת.

lakh-ma-nee-YOT.

588. I will order [an omelet].

אַזְמִין [אוֹמְלֶט *or* חֲבִיתָה].

az-MEEN [om-LET or kha-vee-TAH].

589. —— soft-boiled eggs.

בֵּיצִים רַכּוֹת.

bay-TSEEM ra-KOT.

590. —— a four-minute egg.

בֵּיצָה מְבוּשֶּׁלֶת אַרְבָּעָה רְגָעִים.

bay-TSAH muh-voo-SHEH-let ar-ba-AH ruh-ga-EEM.

591. —— hard-boiled eggs.

בֵּיצִים קָשׁוֹת.

bay-TSEEM ka-SHOT.

592. —— fried egg.

בֵּיצִיָה.

bay-tsee-YAH.

593. —— scrambled eggs.

חֲבִיתָה.

kha-vee-TAH.

SOUPS AND ENTRÉES

מָרָק וּמָנָה רָאשִׁית

594. I want [chicken soup].

אֲבַקֵּשׁ [מָרָק עוֹף].

a-va-KAYSH [ma-RAK of].

595. —— borscht.

חֲמִיצָה.

kha-mee-TSAH.

596. —— fruit soup.

מָרָק פֵּירוֹת.

ma-RAK pay-ROT.

597. —— vegetable soup.

מָרָק יְרָקוֹת.

ma-RAK yuh-ra-KOT.

598. —— beef.

בְּשַׂר בָּקָר.

buh-SAHR ba-KAHR.

599. —— roast beef.

רוֹסְטְבִּיף.

rost-BEEF.

600. —— carp.

קַרְפְּיוֹן.

karp-YON.

601. —— creamed cottage cheese.

גְּבִינָה לְבָנָה.

guh-vee-NAH luh-va-NAH.

602. —— sour cream.

שַׁמֶּנֶת.

sha-MEH-net.

603. —— broiled *or* roast chicken.

עוֹף צָלוּי.

of tsa-LOO-ee.

604. —— fried chicken.

עוֹף מְטֻגָּן.

of muh-tŏŏ-GAN.

605. —— duck.

בַּרְוָז.

bar-VAZ.

606. —— goose.

אַוָּז.

a-VAZ.

607. —— lamb.

בְּשַׂר כֶּבֶשׂ.

buh-SAHR KEH-ves.

608. —— liver.

כָּבֵד.

ka-VAYD.

609. —— pork.

בְּשַׂר חֲזִיר.

buh-SAHR kha-ZEER.

610. —— sardines.

סַרְדִּינִים.

sahr-DEE-neem.

611. —— sausage.

נַקְנִיק.

nak-NEEK.

612. —— shishkebab.

קַבָּב *or* שָׁשְׁלִיק.

ka-BAB or shash-LEEK.

613. —— steak.

סְטֵק *or* אוּמְצָה.

siehk or oom-TSAH.

614. —— veal.

בְּשַׂר עֵגֶל.

buh-SAHR EH-gel.

615. —— a kind of yoghurt.

לֶבֶּן *or* לֶבֶּנִיָּה.

LEH-ben or leh-beh-NEE-ya.

VEGETABLES AND SALAD
יְרָקוֹת וְסָלָט

616. Please serve me some [asparagus].

נָא לְהַגִּישׁ לִי קְצָת [אַסְפָּרַגּוּס].

nah luh-ha-GEESH lee kuh-TSAT [as-pa-RAH-goos].

617. —— beans.

שְׁעוּעִית.

shuh-oo-EET.

618. —— cabbage.

כְּרוּב.

kroov.

619. —— carrots.

גֶּזֶר.

GEH-zehr.

620. —— cauliflower.

כְּרוּבִית.

kroo-VEET.

621. —— cucumber.

מְלָפְפוֹן.

muh-la-fuh-FON.

622. —— cussa, a cucumber-like vegetable.

קִשּׁוּאִים.

kee-shoo-EEM.

623. —— eggplant.

חֲצִילִים.

kha-tsee-LEEM.

624. —— lettuce.

חַסָּה.

KHA-sa.

625. —— mushrooms.

פִּטְרִיּוֹת.

peet-ree-YOT.

626. —— black olives.

זֵיתִים שְׁחוֹרִים.

zay-TEEM shuh-kho-REEM.

627. —— green olives.

זֵיתִים יְרוּקִים.

zay-TEEM yuh-roo-KEEM.

628. —— peas.

אֲפוּנָה.

a-foo-NAH.

629. —— peppers.

פִּלְפְּלִים.

peel-puh-LEEM.

630. —— boiled potatoes.

תַּפּוּחֵי אֲדָמָה מְבוּשָּׁלִים.

ta-poo-KHAY a-da-MAH muh-voo-sha-LEEM.

631. —— fried potatoes.

תַּפּוּחֵי אֲדָמָה מְטוּגָּנִים.

ta-poo-KHAY a da-MAH muh-too-ga-NEEM.

632. —— mashed potatoes.

תַּפּוּחֵי אֲדָמָה מְרוּסָקִים.

ta-poo-KHAY a-da-MAH muh-roo-sa-KEEM.

633. —— rice.

אֹרֶז.

O-rez.

634. —— crushed soya beans.

טְחִינָה.

tuh-KHEE-nah.

635. —— spinach.

תֶּרֶד.

TEH-red.

636. —— tomatoes.

עַגְבָנִיּוֹת.

ag-va-nee-YOT.

637. —— deep fried vegetable balls.

פָלָפֶל.

fa-LA-fel.

FRUIT

פֵּירוֹת

638. Please bring me [an apple].

נָא לְהָבִיא לִי [תַּפּוּחַ].

nah luh-ha-VEE lee [ta-POO-akh].

639. —— apricots.

מִישְׁמֵשׁ.

MEESH-meesh.

640. —— breadfruit (carobs).

חָרוּבִים.

kha-roo-VEEM.

641. —— some cherries.

כַּמָּה דּוּבְדְּבָנִים.

ka-MAH doov-duh-va-NEEM.

642. —— dates.

תְּמָרִים.

tuh-ma-REEM.

643. —— figs.

תְּאֵנִים.

tuh-ay-NEEM.

644. —— a grapefruit.

אֶשְׁכּוֹלִית.

esh-ko-LEET.

645. —— some grapes.

כַּמָּה עֲנָבִים.

ka-MAH a-na-VEEM.

646. —— a lemon.

לִימוֹן.

lee-MON.

647. —— a melon.

אֲבַטִּיחַ.

a-va-TEE-akh.

648. —— mulberries.

תּוּת.

toot.

649. —— an orange.

תַּפּוּחַ זָהָב.

ta-POO-akh za-HAV.

650. —— a peach.

אֲפַרְסֵק.

a-far-SAYK.

651. ——prickly pear.

צַבָּר.

tsa-BAHR.

652. —— raspberries.

פֶּטֶל.

puh-ta-LEEM.

653. —— strawberries.

תּוּת שָׂדֶה.

toot sa-DEH.

BEVERAGES

מַשְׁקָאוֹת

654. I will drink [a cup of black coffee].

אֶשְׁתֶּה [סֵפֶל קָפֶה שָׁחוֹר].

esh-TEH [SEH-fel ka-FEH sha-KHOR].

655. —— coffee with milk.

קָפֶה עִם חָלָב.

ka-FEH eem kha-LAV.

656. —— Turkish coffee.

קָפֶה טוּרְקִי.

ka-FEH toor-KEE.

657. —— a glass of tea.

כּוֹס תֵּה.

kos tay.

658. —— hot chocolate.

קָקָאוֹ חַם.

ka-KA-o kham.

659. —— a glass of milk.

כּוֹס חָלָב.

kos kha-LAV.

660. —— lemonade.

לִימוֹנָדָה.

lee-mo-NA-da.

DESSERTS

מָנוֹת אַחֲרוֹנוֹת

661. May I have some [cake]?

הַאוּכַל לְקַבֵּל [עוּגָה]?

ha-oo-KHAL luh-ka-BAYL [oo-GAH]?

662. —— a fruit cake.

עוּגַת פֵּירוֹת.

oo-GAT pay-ROT.

663. —— cheese.

גְּבִינָה.

guh-vee-NAH.

664. —— cookies.

עוּגִיּוֹת.

oo-gee-YOT.

665. —— custard.

פּוּדִינג.

POO-ding.

666. —— halva.

חַלְבָּה.

khal-VAH.

667. —— chocolate ice cream.

גְּלִידַת שׁוֹקוֹלַדָה.

glee-DAT sho-ko-LA-da.

668. —— vanilla ice cream.

גְּלִידַת וָנִיל.

glee-DAT va-NEEL.

669. —— whipped cream.

שַׁמֶּנֶת קַצֶפֶת.

sha-MEH-net kat-TSEH-fet.

RELIGIOUS SERVICES

עִנְיְנֵי דָּת

670. At what time is the service?

מָתַי הוּא זְמַן הַתְּפִלָּה?

ma-TIE hoo zuh-MAN ha-tuh-fee-LAH?

671. A Catholic Church.

כְּנֵסִיָּה קָטוֹלִית.

kuh-nay-see-YAH ka-TO-leet.

672. A Protestant church.

כְּנֵסִיָּה פְּרוֹטֶסְטַנְטִית.

kuh-nay-see-YAH pro-tes-TAN-teet.

673. A synagogue.

בֵּית כְּנֶסֶת.

bayt KNEH-set.

674. Is there an English-speaking [rabbi] minister *or* priest?

הַאִם יֵשׁ פֹּה [רַב] כּוֹמֶר הַדּוֹבֵר אַנְגְּלִית?

ha-EEM yesh poh [rav] ko-MAR ha-do-VAYR ang-LEET?

SIGHTSEEING

סִיּוּר

675. Where can I rent [a car]?

אֵיפֹה אוּכַל לִשְׂכּוֹר [מְכוֹנִית]?

ay-FOH oo-KHAL lees-KOR [muh-kho-NEET] ?

676. —— a bicycle.

אוֹפַנַּיִם.

of-NAH-yeem.

677. —— a horse and carriage.

סוּס וַעֲגָלָה.

soos va-a-ga-LAH.

678. I want a licensed guide who speaks English.

אֲנִי (רוֹצֶה) (רוֹצָה) מוֹרֶה דֶּרֶךְ בַּעַל רִשָּׁיוֹן הַמְּדַבֵּר אַנְגְלִית.

a-NEE (ro-TSEH, M.) (ro-TSAH, F.) mo-REH DEH-rekh BA-al ree-sha-YON ha-muh-da-BAYR ang-LEET.

679. What is the charge [per hour] per day?

מַה הַמְּחִיר [לְשָׁעָה] לְיוֹם?

mah ha-muh-KHEER [luh-sha-AH] luh-YOM?

680. What is the fare for a trip [to the collective farm]?

כַּמָּה תַּעֲלֶה הַנְּסִיעָה [לַקִּבּוּץ]?

ka-MAH ta-a-LEH ha-nuh-see-AH [la-kee-BOOTS]?

681. —— to the mountains.

לֶהָרִים.

leh-ha-REEM.

682. —— on the river.

עַל הַנָּהָר.

al ha-na-HAHR.

683. —— to the sea.

לַיָּם.

la-YAM.

684. Call for me at my hotel at 8 o'clock.

(בֹּא) לָקַחַת אוֹתִי בַּמָּלוֹן שֶׁלִּי בְּשָׁעָה שְׁמֹנֶה.

(bo, TO M.) *la-KA-khat o-TEE ba-ma-LON sheh-LEE buh-sha-AH SHMO-neh.*

685. Please show me all the sights of interest.

אֲבַקֵּשׁ לְהַרְאוֹת לִי אֶת כָּל הַדְּבָרִים הַמְעַנְיְנִים.

a-va-KAYSH luh-har-OT lee et kol ha-dva-REEM ha-muh-an-yuh-NEEM.

686. I am interested in architecture.

אֲנִי (מְעוּנְיָן) (מְעוּנְיֶנֶת) בְּאַרְכִיטֶקְטוּרָה.

a-NEE (muh-oon-YAN, M.) *(muh-oon-YEH-net,* F.) *buh-ar-khee-tek-TOO-ra.*

687. Painting.

צִיּוּר.

tsee-YOOR.

688. Sculpture.

פִּסּוּל.

pee-SOOL.

689. Native arts and crafts.

אֲמָנוּת וּמְלֶאכֶת יַד מְקוֹמִית.

o-ma-NOOT oo-muh-LEH-khet yad muh-ko-MEET.

690. Archaeology.

אַרְכֵיאוֹלוֹגְיָה.

ar-khee-o-LOG-ya.

691. I would like to visit [the park].

בִּרְצוֹנִי לְבַקֵּר [בַּגַּן הַצִּבּוּרִי].

beer-tso-NEE luh-va-KAYR [ba-GAN ha-tsee-boo-REE].

692. —— the cathedral.

הַכְּנֵסִיָּה.

ha-knay-see-YAH.

693. —— the castle.

הָאַרְמוֹן.

ha-ar-MON.

694. —— the library.

הַסִּפְרִיָּה.

ha-seef-ree-YAH.

695. —— the monument.

הַמַּצֵּבָה.

ha-ma-tsay-VAH.

696. —— the parliament.

הַכְּנֶסֶת.

ha-KNEH-set.

697. When does the museum [open] close?

מָתַי [פּוֹתְחִים] סוֹגְרִים אֶת בֵּית הַנְּכֹאת?

ma-TIE [pot-KHEEM] sog-REEM et bayt ha-nuh-KHOT?

698. Is this the way to [the entrance] the exit?

הַאִם זוֹ הִיא הַדֶּרֶךְ [לַכְּנִיסָה] לַיְצִיאָה?

ha-EEM zoh hee ha-DEH-rekh [la-kuh-nee-SAH] la-yuh-tsee-AH?

699. What is the price of admission?

מַה דְּמֵי הַכְּנִיסָה?

mah duh-MAY ha-kuh-nee-SAH?

700. We would like to stop and see the view for a minute.

אֲנַחְנוּ רוֹצִים לַעֲמוֹד לְרֶגַע וְלִרְאוֹת אֶת הַנּוֹף.

a-NAKH-noo ro-TSEEM la-a-MOD luh-REH-ga vuh-leer-OT et ha-NOF.

701. Take us back to the hotel, please.

(הַחֲזֵר) אוֹתָנוּ לַמָּלוֹן, בְּבַקָשָׁה.

(ha-kha-ZAYR, то м.) o-TAH-noo la-ma-LON, buh-va-ka-SHAH.

702. If we have time, we shall visit the art gallery.

אִם יֵשׁ לָנוּ זְמַן נְבַקֵּר בַּמּוֹזֵיאוֹן.

eem yesh LAH-noo zman nuh-va-KAYR ba-moo-ZAY-on.

AMUSEMENTS

שַׁעֲשׁוּעִים

703. I would like to go to a concert.

בִּרְצוֹנִי לְבַקֵּר בְּקוֹנְצֶרְט.

beer-tso-NEE luh-va-KAYR buh-kon-TSEHRT.

704. The ballet.

הַבָּלֶט.

ha-ba-LET.

705. The box office.

הַקֻּפָּה.

ha-koo-PAH.

706. The movies.

הַקּוֹלְיוֹעַ.

ha-kol-NO-a.

707. Folk dances.

רִקּוּדֵי עָם.

ree-koo-DAY am.

708. A night club.

מוֹעֲדוֹן לַיְלָה.

mo-a-DON LIE-la.

709. The opera.

הָאוֹפֶּרָה.

ha-O-peh-ra.

710. The theatre.

הַתֵּאַטְרוֹן.

ha-tay-a-TRON.

711. What is playing tonight?

מָה מַצִּיגִים חָעֶרֶב?

mah ma-tsee-GEEM ha-EH-rev?

712. Is there a matinee performance today?

הַאִם יֵשׁ הַצָּגָה יוֹמִית הַיּוֹם?

ha-EEM yesh ha-tsa-GAH yo-MEET ha-YOM?

713. Are there any seats for tonight?

הַאִם יֵשׁ מְקוֹמוֹת לְהָעֶרֶב?

ha-EEM yesh muh-ko-MOT luh-ha-EH-rev?

714. How much is [an orchestra seat]?

כַּמָּה עוֹלֶה [מָקוֹם בָּאוּלָם]?

ka-MAH o-LEH [ma-KOM bah-oo-LAM]?

715. —— a balcony seat.

מָקוֹם בַּיָצִיעַ.

ma-KOM ba-ya-TSEE-a.

716. —— a box.

תָּא מְיֻחָד.

ta muh-yoo-KHAD.

717. May I have a program?

הַאוּכַל לְקַבֵּל תָּכְנִית?

ha-oo-KHAL luh-ka-BAYL tokh-NEET?

718. Can I rent opera glasses?

הַאוּכַל לִשְׂכּוֹר מִשְׁקֶפֶת אוֹפֶּרָה?

ha-oo-KHAL lees-KOR meesh-KEH-fet O-peh-ra?

719. Not [too near] too far from the stage.

לֹא [קָרוֹב מִדַּי] רָחוֹק מִדַּי מֵהַבָּמָה.

loh [ka-ROV mee-DIE] ra-KHOK mee-DIE may-ha-ba-MAH.

720. Will I be able to [see] hear well?

הַאוּכַל [לִרְאוֹת] לִשְׁמוֹעַ הֵיטֵב?

ha-oo-KHAL [leer-OT] leesh-MO-a hay-TAYV?

721. What are you doing tonight?

מָה (אַתָּה עוֹשֶׂה) (אַתְּ עוֹשָׂה) הָעֶרֶב?

mah (a-TAH o-SEH TO M.) (at o-SAH, TO F.) ha-EH-rev?

722. When does the evening performance begin?

מָתַי תַּתְחִיל הַצָּגַת הָעֶרֶב?

ma-TIE tat-KHEEL ha-tsa-GAT ha-EH-rev?

723. How long is the intermission?

כַּמָּה זְמַן יֵשׁ הַפְסָקָה?

ka-MAH zman yesh haf-sa-KAH?

724. The show was [interesting] funny.

הַהַצָּגָה הָיְתָה [מְעַנְיֶנֶת] מַצְחִיקָה.

ha-ha-tsa-GAH hie-TAH [muh-an-YEH-net] mats-khee-KAH.

725. Where can we go to dance?

אֵיפֹה אֶפְשָׁר לָלֶכֶת לִרְקוֹד?

ay-FOH ef-SHAHR la-LEH-khet leer-KOD?

726. May I have this dance?

הַאִם אֶפְשָׁר (לְהַזְמִינֵךְ) לָרְקוֹד הַזֶּה?

ha-EEM ef-SHAHR (luh-haz-mee-NEKH, TO F.) la-ree-KOOD ha-ZEH?

727. Will you play [a fox trot]?

הַאִם תּוּכְלוּ לְנַגֵּן [פוֹקְסְטרוֹט]?

ha-EEM tookh-LOO luh-na-GAYN ["fox-trot"]?

728. —— a mambo.

מַמְבּוֹ.

MAM-bo.

729. —— a rumba.

רוּמְבָּה.

ROOM-ba.

730. —— a samba.

סַמְבָּה.

SAM-ba.

731. —— a tango.

טַנְגּוֹ.

TAN-go.

732. —— a waltz.

וַלְץ.

valts.

733. The music is excellent.

הַמּוּזִיקָה מְצוּיֶנֶת.

ha-MOO-zee-ka muh-tsoo-YEH-net.

SPORTS

סְפּוֹרְט

734. Let's go [to the beach].

נֵלֵךְ [לִשְׂפַת הַיָּם].

neh-LEKH [lees-FAT ha-YAM].

735. —— to the swimming pool.

לַבְּרֵכָה.

la-bray-KHAH.

736. —— to the soccer game.

לְמִשְׂחָק כַּדּוּרֶגֶל.

luh-mees-KHAK ka-doo-REH-gel.

737. —— to the horse races.

לְמֵרוּץ הַסּוּסִים.

luh-may-ROOTS ha-soo-SEEM.

738. I'd like to play tennis.

אֲנִי (רוֹצֶה) (רוֹצָה) לְשַׂחֵק טֶנִיס.

a-NEE (ro-TSEH, M.) (ro-TSAH, F.) luh-sa-KHAYK TEH-nees.

739. I need [some golf clubs].

יֵשׁ לִי צֹרֶךְ [בְּמַקְלוֹת גוֹלְף].

yesh lee TSO-rekh [buh-mak-LOT golf].

740. —— a tennis racket.

רָקֶטָה לְטֶנִיס.

ra-KEH-ta luh-TEH-nees.

741. —— some fishing tackle.

כְּלֵי דַיִג.

klay DAH-yeeg.

742. Can we go [fishing]?

הַאִם נוּכַל לָלֶכֶת [לָדוּג]?

ha-EEM noo-KHAL la-LEH-khet [la-DOOG] ?

743. —— horseback riding.

לִרְכַּב.

leer-KAV.

744. —— swimming.

לִשְׂחוֹת.

lees-KHOT.

BANK AND MONEY

בַּנְק וְכֶסֶף

745. Where is the nearest bank?

אֵיפֹה הַבַּנְק הַקָּרוֹב בְּיוֹתֵר?

ay-FOH ha-BANK ha-ka-ROV buh-yo-TAYR?

746. At which window can I cash this?

בְּאֵיזֶה חַלוֹן אֲקַבֵּל זֶה?

buh-AY-zeh kha-LON a-ka-BAYL zeh?

747. Will you cash a check?

הֲתִפְרְטוּ הַמְחָאָה?

ha-teef-ruh-TOO ham-kha-AH?

748. I have [travelers' checks].

יֵשׁ לִי [הַמְחָאוֹת תַּיָרִים].

yesh lee [ham-kha-OT ta-ya-REEM].

749. —— a bank draft.

הַמְחָאַת בַּנְק.

ham-kha-AT bank.

750. —— a letter of credit.

אִגֶּרֶת אַשְׁרַאי.

ee-GEH-ret ash-ra-EE.

751. —— a credit card.

כַּרְטִיס אַשְׁרַאי.

kar-TEES ash-ra-EE.

752. What is the exchange rate on the dollar?

מַהוּ שַׁעַר הַחֲלִיפִין שֶׁל הַדּוֹלָר?

mah-HOO SHAH-ar ha-kha-lee-FEEN shel ha-doh-LAHR?

753. May I have thirty dollars' worth of pounds?

הַאוּכַל לְקַבֵּל לִירוֹת בְּעֶרֶךְ שֶׁל שְׁלוֹשִׁים דּוֹלָר?

ha-oo-KHAL luh-ka-BAYL LEE-rot buh-EH-rekh shel shlo-SHEEM doh-LAHR?

754. Please change this [for some large bills].

אֲבַקֵּשׁ לְהַחֲלִיף זֹאת [לִשְׁטָרוֹת גְּדוֹלִים].

a-va-KAYSH luh-ha-kha-LEEF zot [leesh-ta-ROT guh-doh-LEEM].

755. —— for some small bills.

לִשְׁטָרוֹת קְטַנִּים.

leesh-ta-ROT kuh-ta-NEEM.

756. —— for some small change.

לְכֶסֶף קָטָן.

luh-KHEH-sef ka-TAN.

757. I want to send fifty dollars to the U.S.

אֲבַקֵּשׁ לִשְׁלוֹחַ חֲמִשִּׁים דּוֹלָר לְאַרְצוֹת הַבְּרִית.

a-va-KAYSH leesh-LO-akh kha-mee-SHEEM doh-LAHR luh-ar-TSOT ha-BREET.

SHOPPING

קְנִיוֹת

758. I want to go shopping.

אֲנִי (רוֹצֶה) (רוֹצָה) לַעֲשׂוֹת קְנִיוֹת.

a-NEE (ro-TSEH, M.) (ro-TSAH, F.) la-a-SOT kuh-nee-YOT.

759. Please take me to the shopping center.

נָא לָקַחַת אוֹתִי לַחֲנוּיוֹת.

nah la-KA-khat o-TEE la-kha-noo-YOT.

760. May I speak to a [salesman] salesgirl?

הַאוּכַל לְדַבֵּר עִם [מוֹכֵר] מוֹכֶרֶת?

ha-oo-KHAL luh-da-BAYR eem [mo-KHAYR] mo-KHEH-ret?

761. Is there anyone here who speaks English?

הַאִם יֵשׁ פֹּה מִישֶׁהוּ שֶׁמְּדַבֵּר אַנְגְּלִית?

ha-EEM yesh poh MEE-shuh-hoo shuh-muh-da-BAYR ang-LEET?

762. I only want to look around.

אֲנִי רַק (רוֹצֶה) (רוֹצָה) לִרְאוֹת.

a-NEE rak (ro-TSEH, M.) (ro-TSAH, F.) leer-OT.

763. Sale.

מְכִירָה.

muh-khee-RAH.

764. How much is it [for each piece]?

כַּמָּה זֶה עוֹלֶה [כָּל אֶחָד]?

ka-MAH zeh o-LEH [kol eh-KHAD]?

765. —— per meter.

כָּל מֶטֶר.

kol MEH-tehr.

766. —— all together.

כּוּלָם יַחַד.

koo-LAM YA-khad.

767. It is too expensive.

זֶה יָקָר מִדַּי.

zeh ya-KAHR mee-DIE.

768. Is that the lowest price?

הַאִם זֶה הוּא הַמְּחִיר הַנָּמוּךְ בְּיוֹתֵר?

ha-EEM ZEH*hoo ha-muh-KHEER ha-na-MOOKH
buh-yo-TAYR?

769. Is there [a discount] a guarantee?

יֵשׁ [הֲנָחָה] אַחֲרָיוּת?

yesh [ha-na-KHAH] a-kha-ra-YOOT?

770. The price is satisfactory.

הַמְּחִיר הוּא בְּסֵדֶר.

ha-muh-KHEER hoo buh-SEH-dehr.

771. I do not like that.

זֶה לֹא מוֹצֵא חֵן בְּעֵינַי.

zeh loh mo-TSAY khen buh-ay-NIE.

772. I prefer something better.

אֲנִי (רוֹצֶה) (רוֹצָה) מַשֶּׁהוּ יוֹתֵר טוֹב.

a-NEE (ro-TSEH, м.) (ro-TSAH, ꜰ.) MAH-shuh-
hoo yo-TAYR tov.

773. Cheaper.

יוֹתֵר זוֹל.

yo-TAYR zoll.

774. At a moderate price.

בְּמְחִיר בֵּינוֹנִי.

beem-KHEER bay-no-NEE.

775. Finer.

יוֹתֵר עָדִין.

yo-TAYR a-DEEN.

776. Plainer.

יוֹתֵר פָּשׁוּט.

yo-TAYR pa-SHOOT.

777. Softer.

יוֹתֵר רַךְ.

yo-TAYR rakh.

778. Stronger.

יוֹתֵר חָזָק.

yo-TAYR kha-ZAK.

779. Looser.

יוֹתֵר רָחָב.

yo-TAYR ra-KHAV.

780. Tighter.

יוֹתֵר צַר.

yo-TAYR tsahr.

781. Of medium size.

בְּגֹדֶל בֵּינוֹנִי.

buh-GO-del bay-no-NEE.

782. Show me some others in a different style.

(הַרְאֵה) (הַרְאִי) לִי עוֹד אֲחֵרִים בְּסִגְנוֹן אַחֵר.

(har-AY, TO M.) (har-EE, TO F.) lee od a-khay-REEM buh-seeg-NON a-KHAYR.

783. May I try this on?

הַאוּכַל לְנַסּוֹת אֶת זֶה?

ha-oo-KHAL luh-na-SOT et zeh?

784. Will it [fade] shrink?

הַאִם זֶה [יִדְהֶה] יִתְכַּוֵּץ?

ha-EEM zeh [yeed-HEH] yeet-ka-VAYTS?

785. It is not becoming to me.

זֶה לֹא הוֹלֵם אוֹתִי.

zeh toh ho-LAYM o-TEE.

786. It does not fit me.

זֶה לֹא מַתְאִים לִי.

zeh loh mat-EEM lee.

787. May I order one?

הַאוּכַל לְהַזְמִין אֶחָד?

ha-oo-KHAL luh-haz-MEEN eh-KHAD?

788. How long will the alterations take?

כַּמָּה זְמַן יִקְחוּ הַשִּׁנּוּיִים?

ka-MAH zman yeek-KHOO ha-shee-noo-YEEM?

789. I shall come back [later] soon.

אֶחֱזוֹר [אַחַר כָּךְ] עוֹד מְעַט.

a-kha-ZOR [a-KHAHR-kakh] od muh-AT.

790. Please wrap this.

אֲבַקֵּשׁ לַעֲטוֹף זֹאת.

a-va-KAYSH la-a-TOF zot.

791. I shall take it with me.

אֶקַּח אֶת זֶה אִתִּי.

eh-KAKH et zeh ee-TEE.

792. Whom do I pay, the cashier?

לְמִי עָלַי לְשַׁלֵּם, לַקּוּפַּאי?

luh-MEE a-LIE luh-sha-LAYM, la-koo-pa-EE?

793. Can it be delivered to my hotel?

הַאִם אֶפְשָׁר לִשְׁלוֹחַ לִי זֹאת לַמָּלוֹן?

ha-EEM ef-SHAHR leesh-LO-akh lee zot la-ma-LON?

794. It is fragile.

זֶה שָׁבִיר.

zeh sha-VEER.

795. Pack it for export.

אֲבַקֵּשׁ לֶאֱרֹז אֶת זֶה בִּשְׁבִיל אֶקְסְפּוֹרְט.

a-va-KAYSH leh-eh-ROZ et zeh beesh-VEEL eks-PORT.

796. Ship it by freight to Philadelphia.

תִּשְׁלְחוּ זֹאת כִּסְחוֹרָה לְפִילָדֶלְפִּיָה.

teesh-luh-KHOO zot kuh-skho-RAH luh-fee-la-DEL-fya.

797. Please give me [a bill].

אֲבַקֵּשׁ [חֶשְׁבּוֹן].

a-va-KAYSH [khesh-BON].

798. —— a receipt *or* sales slip.

קַבָּלָה.

ka-ba-LAH.

799. I shall pay when it is delivered.

אֲשַׁלֵּם כְּשֶׁזֶּה יִתְקַבֵּל.

a-sha-LAYM kuh-shuh-ZEH yeet-ka-BAYL.

800. Are there any other charges?

הַאִם יֵשׁ עוֹד תַּשְׁלוּמִים אֲחֵרִים?

ha-EEM yesh od tash-loo-MEEM a-khay-REEM?

MEASUREMENTS

הַמְּדּוֹת

801. Please take my measurements.

נָא לָקַחַת אֶת הַמְּדּוֹת שֶׁלִּי.

nah la-KA-khat et ha-mee-DOT sheh-LEE.

802. What is [the size]?

מַהוּ [הַגֹּדֶל]?

MA-hoo [ha-GO-del]?

803. —— the length.

הָאֹרֶךְ.

ha-O-rekh.

804. —— the width.

הָרֹחַב.

ha-RO-khav.

805. —— the weight.

הַמִּשְׁקָל.

ha-meesh-KAL.

806. It is 7 meters long by 4 meters wide.

זֶה שִׁבְעָה מֶטֶר אֹרֶךְ עַל אַרְבָּעָה מֶטֶר רֹחַב.

zeh sheev-AH MEH-tehr O-rekh al ar-ba-AH MEH-tehr RO-khav.

807. [Small] smaller.*

[קָטָן] יוֹתֵר קָטָן.

[ka-TAN] yo-TAYR ka-TAN.

---

* The comparative form (-er) is expressed in Hebrew by adding the word יוֹתֵר (more) to the adjective. It can be used either before or after the adjective. The superlative form (-est) is formed by adding בְּיוֹתֵר (most) after the adjective.

808. Large.

גָּדוֹל.

ga-DOL.

809. High.

גָּבוֹהַ.

ga-VO-hah.

810. Low.

נָמוּךְ.

na-MOOKH.

811. Long.

אָרוֹךְ.

a-ROKH.

812. Short.

קָצָר.

ka-TSAHR.

813. Thin.

דַּק.

dak.

814. Thick.

עָבֶה.

a-VEH.

815. Narrow.

צַר.

tsahr.

816. Wide.

רָחָב.

ra-KHAHV.

817. Old.

יָשָׁן.

ya-SHAN.

818. New.

חָדָשׁ.

kha-DASH.

COLORS

צְבָעִים

819. I want something [lighter] darker.

אֲבַקֵשׁ מַשֶּׁהוּ [יוֹתֵר בָּהִיר] יוֹתֵר כֵּהֶה.

a-va-KAYSH MAH-shuh-hoo [yo-TAYR ba-HEER yo-TAYR kay-HEH.

820. Color.

צֶבַע.

TSEH-va.

821. Black.

שָׁחוֹר.

sha-KHOR.

822. Blue.

כָּחוֹל.

ka-KHOL.

823. Brown.

חוּם.

khoom.

824. Cream.

קְרֶם.

kraym.

825. Gray.

אָפוֹר.

a-FOR.

826. Green.

יָרֹק.

ya-ROK.

827. Orange.

כָּתֹם.

ka-TOM.

828. Pink.

וָרֹד.

va-ROD.

829. Purple.

אַרְגָּמָן.

ar-ga-MAN.

830. Red.

אָדֹם.

a-DOM.

831. White.

לָבָן.

la-VAN.

832. Yellow.

צָהֹב.

tsa-HOV.

STORES

חֲנֻיּוֹת

833. Where do I find [an antique shop]?

אֵיפֹה אֶמְצָא [חֲנוּת עַתִּיקוֹת]?

ay-FOH em-TSA [kha-NOOT a-tee-KOT]?

834. —— a bakery,
מַאֲפִיָּה.
ma-a-fee-YAH.

835. —— a book shop.
חֲנוּת סְפָרִים.
kha-NOOT sfa-REEM.

836. —— a butcher *or* meat market.
קַצָּב.
ka-TSAV.

837. —— a candy store.
חֲנוּת מַמְתַּקִּים.
kha-NOOT mam-ta-KEEM.

838. —— a cigar store.
חֲנוּת סִיגָרִיּוֹת.
kha-NOOT see-ga-ree-YOT.

839. —— a clothing store.
חֲנוּת הַלְבָּשָׁה.
kha-NOOT hal-ba-SHAH.

840. —— a department store *or* five and dime store.
חֲנוּת כָּל־בּוֹ.
kha-NOOT kol-BO.

841. —— a dressmaker.
תּוֹפֶרֶת.
to-FEH-ret.

842. —— a drug store *or* pharmacy.
בֵּית מִרְקַחַת.
bayt meer-KA-khat.

843. —— a dry goods store *or* haberdashery.

גָּלַנְטֶרְיָה.

ga-lan-TEHR-yah.

844. —— a florist.

חֲנוּת פְּרָחִים.

kha-NOOT pra-KHEEM.

845. —— a fruit and vegetable store.

חֲנוּת לִירָקוֹת וּפֵירוֹת.

kha-NOOT lee-ra-KOT oo-fay-ROT.

846. —— a grocery.

חֲנוּת מַכֹּלֶת.

kha-NOOT ma-KO-let.

847. —— a hardware store.

חֲנוּת כְּלֵי בַּיִת.

kha-NOOT klay BA-yeet.

848. —— a hat shop *or* milliner.

חֲנוּת כּוֹבָעִים.

kha-NOOT ko-va-EEM.

849. —— a jewelry store *or* jeweler.

צוֹרֵף.

tso-RAYF.

850. —— a liquor store.

חֲנוּת לְמַשְׁקָאוֹת חֲרִיפִים.

kha-NOOT luh-mash-ka-OT kha-ree-FEEM.

851. —— a market.

שׁוּק.

shook.

852. —— a music shop.

חֲנוּת לִכְלֵי נְגִינָה.

kha-NOOT leekh-LAY nuh-gee-NAH.

853. —— a shoemaker.

סַנְדְּלָר.

san-DLAHR.

854. —— a shoe repair shop.

סַנְדְּלָרִיָה.

san-dla-ree-YAH.

855. —— a shoe store.

חֲנוּת נַעֲלַיִם.

kha-NOOT nuh-a-LAH-yeem.

856. —— a tailor.

חַיָּט.

kha-YAT.

857. —— a toy shop.

חֲנוּת צַעֲצוּעִים.

kha-NOOT tsa-a-tsoo-EEM.

858. —— a watchmaker.

שָׁעָן.

sha-AN.

CIGAR STORE

חֲנוּת סִיגָרִיּוֹת

859. Is the cigar store open?

הַאִם חֲנוּת הַסִּיגָרִיּוֹת פְּתוּחָה?

ha-EEM kha-NOOT ha-see-ga-ree-YOT puh-too-KHAH?

860. I want to buy some cigars.

אֲנִי (רוֹצֶה) (רוֹצָה) לִקְנוֹת כַּמָּה סִיגָרוֹת.

a-NEE (ro-TSEH, M.) (ro-TSAH, F.) leek-NOT ka-MAH see-GA-rot.

861. A pack of American cigarettes.

קוּפְסַת סִיגָרִיּוֹת אֲמֶרִיקָאִיּוֹת.

koof-SAT see-ga-ree-YOT a-meh-ree-KA-ee-yot.

862. A cigarette case.

נַרְתִּיק לְסִיגָרִיּוֹת.

nar-TEEK luh-see-ga-ree-YOT.

863. A pipe.

מִקְטֶרֶת.

meek-TEH-ret.

864. Pipe tobacco.

טַבַּק לְמִקְטֶרֶת.

ta-BAK luh-meek-TEH-ret.

865. A lighter.

מַצִּית.

ma-TSEET.

866. Lighter fluid.

דֶּלֶק לְמַצִּית.

DEH-lek luh-ma-TSEET.

867. A flint.

אֶבֶן אֵשׁ.

eh-ven AYSH.

DRUGSTORE

בֵּית מִרְקַחַת

868. Where is there a drugstore where they understand English?

אֵיפֹה יֵשׁ בֵּית מִרְקַחַת בּוֹ מְבִינִים אַנְגְלִית?

ay-FOH yesh bayt meer-KA-khat bo muh-vee-NEEM ang-LEET?

869. Can you fill this prescription immediately?

הַאִם אֶפְשָׁר לְהָכִין אֶת פֶּתֶק הָרְפוּאָה הַזֶּה תֵּכֶף?

*ha-EEM ef-SHAHR luh-ha-KHEEN et PEH-tek
har-foo-AH ha-zeh TAY-khef?*

870. Do you have [adhesive tape]?

יֵשׁ לָכֶם [סֶרֶט דּוֹבֵק]?

yesh la-khem [SEH-ret do-VAYK]?

871. —— alcohol.

אַלְכּוֹהוֹל.

al-ko-HOL.

872. —— antiseptic.

אַנְטִיסֶפְּטִיק.

an-tee-SEP-teek.

873. —— aspirin.

אַסְפִּירִין.

as-pee-REEN.

874. —— bandages.

תַּחְבּוֹשׁוֹת.

takh-bo-SHOT.

875. —— bicarbonate of soda.

אַבְקַת סוֹדָה.

av-KAT SO-da.

876. —— boric acid.

מֵי בּוֹרִית.

may bo-REET.

877. —— a jar of cold cream.

צִנְצֶנֶת מִשְׁחַת פָּנִים.

tseen-TSEH-net meesh-KHAT pa-NEEM.

878. —— a comb.

מַסְרֵק.

mas-RAYK.

879. —— corn pads.

מַדְבֵּקוֹת לְיַבָּלוֹת.

mad bay-KOT luh-ya-ba-LOT.

880. —— a deodorant.

מוֹנֵעַ רֵיחַ.

mo-NEH-a RAY-akh.

881. —— a depilatory.

מֵסִיר שֵׂעָר.

may-SEER say-AHR.

882. —— ear stoppers.

סוֹתְמֵי אָזְנַיִם.

sot-MAY oz-NAH-yeem.

883. —— an eye-cup or eye-bath.

אַמְבַּטְיַת עַיִן.

am-BAT-yat AH-yeen.

884. —— a box of face tissues.

קוּפְסַת מַגְבוֹת נְיָר לַפָּנִים.

koof-SAT ma-ga-VOT nyahr luh-pa-NEEM.

885. —— gauze.

גָּזָה.

GA-za.

886. —— hand lotion.

מִשְׁחַת יָדַיִם.

meesh-KHAT ya-DAH-yeem.

887. —— a hairbrush.

מִבְרֶשֶׁת שֵׂעָר.

meev-REH-shet say-AHR.

888. —— hairpins.

סִכּוֹת רֹאשׁ.

see-KOT rosh.

889. —— a hot water bottle.

בַּקְבּוּק חַם.

bak-BOOK kham.

890. —— an ice-bag.

שַׂקִּית קֶרַח.

sa-KEET KEH-rakh.

891. —— insect repellent.

מִשְׁחָה נֶגֶד יַתּוּשִׁים.

meesh-KHAH NEH-ged yee-too-SHEEM.

892. —— iodine.

יוֹד.

yod.

893. —— a laxative.

רְפוּאָה מְשַׁלְשֶׁלֶת.

ruh-foo-AH muh-shal-SHEH-let.

894. —— a lipstick.

אֹדֶם שְׂפָתַיִם.

O-dem sfa-TAH-yeem.

895. —— a medicine dropper.

מְטַפְטֵף.

muh-taf-TAYF.

896. —— a mouthwash.

מֵי פֶּה.

may-PEH.

897. —— a nail file.

מַבְרֵד צִפָּרְנַיִם.

mav-RAYD tsee-por-NAH-yeem.

898. —— nailpolish.

לַק לַצִּפָּרְנַיִם.

lak luh-tsee-por-NAH-yeem.

899. —— nailpolish remover.

אַצֶטוֹן.

a-tseh-TON.

900. —— hydrogen peroxide.

מֵי פֶּרוֹקְסִיד.

may peh-rok-SEED.

901. —— face powder.

אַבְקַת פָּנִים *or* פּוּדְרָה.

av-KAT pa-NEEM or POOD-ra.

902. —— talcum powder.

אַבְקַת טַלְק,

av-KAT talk.

903. —— a razor.

תַּעַר.

TAH-ar.

904. —— a package of razor blades.

חֲבִילַת סַכִּינֵי גִּלּוּחַ.

kha-vee-LAT sa-kee-NAY gee-LOO-akh.

905. —— rouge.

אֹדֶם לְחָיַיִם.

O-dem leh-kha-YAH-yeem.

906. —— safety pins.

סִכּוֹת בְּטָחוֹן.

see-KOT bee-ta-KHON.

907. —— sanitary napkins.

תַּחְבּשׁוֹת נָשִׁים.

takh-bo-SHOT na-SHEEM.

908. —— a sedative.

רְפוּאָה מַרְגִּעַת.

ruh-foo-AH mar-GAH-at.

909. —— shampoo.

שַׁמְפּוֹן.

sham-PON.

910. —— shaving cream.

סַבּוֹן גִּלּוּחַ.

sa-BON gee-LOO-akh.

911. —— shaving lotion.

מִשְׁחַת גִּלּוּחַ.

meesh-KHAT gee-LOO-akh.

912. —— smelling salts.

מִלְחֵי רֵיחַ.

meel-KHAY RAY-akh.

913. —— a bar of soap.

חֲתִיכַת סַבּוֹן.

kha-tee-KHAT sa-BON.

914. —— soap flakes.

פְּתִיתֵי סַבּוֹן.

puh-tee-TAY sa-BON.

915. ——— a pair of sunglasses.

מִשְׁקְפֵי שֶׁמֶשׁ.

meesh-kuh-FAY SHEH-mesh.

916 ——— sunburn ointment.

מִשְׁחָה נֶגֶד כְּוִיַּת שֶׁמֶשׁ.

meesh-KHAH NEH-ged kvee-YAT SHEH-mesh.

917. ——— suntan oil.

שֶׁמֶן לְשִׁזּוּף.

SHEH-men luh-shee-ZOOF.

918. ——— a thermometer.

מַדְחֹם.

mad-KHOM.

919. ——— a toothbrush.

מִבְרֶשֶׁת שִׁנַּיִם.

meev-REH-shet shee-NAH-yeem.

920. ——— toothpaste.

מִשְׁחַת שִׁנַּיִם.

meesh-KHAT shee-NAH-yeem.

921. ——— a can of toothpowder.

קֻפְסַת אַבְקַת שִׁנַּיִם.

koof-SAT av-KAT shee-NAH-yeem.

CLOTHING STORE

חֲנוּת הַלְבָּשָׁה

922. I want to buy a bathing cap.

אֲנִי (רוֹצֶה) (רוֹצָה) לִקְנוֹת כּוֹבַע יָם.

a-NEE (ro-TSEH, M.) (ro-TSAH, F.) leek-NOT KO-va yam.

923. A bathing suit.

בֶּגֶד יָם.

BEH-ged yam.

924. A blouse.

חֻלְצָה.

khool-TSAH.

925. A brassière.

חֲזִיָּה.

kha-zee-YAH.

926. A coat.

מְעִיל.

muh-EEL.

927. A collar.

צַוָּארוֹן.

tsa-va-RON.

928. Diapers.

חִתּוּלִים.

khee-too-LEEM.

929. A dress.

שִׂמְלָה.

seem-LAH.

930. Children's clothes.

בִּגְדֵי יְלָדִים.

beeg-DAY yuh-la-DEEM.

931. A pair of garters.

זוּג בְּרִיּוֹת.

zoog bee-ree-YOT.

932. A girdle *or* belt.
חֲגוֹרָה.
kha-go-RAH.

933. A pair of gloves.
זוּג כְּפָפוֹת.
zoog kfa-FOT.

934. A handbag.
אַרְנָק.
ar-NAK.

935. A few handkerchiefs.
כַּמָּה מִמְחָטוֹת.
ka-MAH meem-kha-TOT.

936. A hat.
כּוֹבַע.
KO-va.

937. A fur jacket.
מְעִיל פַּרְוָה.
muh-EEL par-VAH.

938. Neckties.
עֲנִיבוֹת.
a-nee-VOT.

939. A nightgown.
כֻּתֹּנֶת לַיְלָה.
koo-TO-net LIE-la.

940. Panties *or* shorts.
תַּחְתּוֹנִים.
takh-to-NEEM.

941. Pajamas.

פִּיזָ'מָה.

pee-JAH-ma.

942. A raincoat.

מְעִיל גֶּשֶׁם.

muh-EEL GEH-shem.

943. A robe *or* dressing gown.

חָלוּק *or* שִׂמְלַת בַּיִת.

khah-LOOK or seem-LAT BAH-yeet.

944. A scarf.

סוּדָר.

soo-DAHR.

945. A pair of shoes.

זוּג נַעֲלַיִם.

zoog nuh-a-LAH-yeem.

946. Shoelaces.

שְׂרוֹכֵי נַעֲלַיִם.

sro-KHAY nuh-a-LAH-yeem.

947. A skirt.

חֲצָאִית.

kha-tsa-EET.

948. A petticoat *or* underskirt.

תַּחְתּוֹנָה.

takh-to-NAH.

949. A pair of slippers.

זוּג נַעֲלֵי בַּיִת.

zoog nuh-a-LAY BAH-yeet.

950. A half-dozen pairs of socks *or* stockings.

חֲצִי תְּרֵיסַר זוּגוֹת גַּרְבַּיִם.

kha-TSEE tray-SAHR zoo-GOT gar-BAH-yeem.

951. A pair of nylon stockings.

זוּג גַּרְבֵּי נַיְילוֹן.

zoog gar-BAY NIE-lon.

952. A suit.

חֲלִיפָה.

kha-lee-FAH.

953. A pair of suspenders.

זוּג כְּתֵפִיּוֹת.

zoog kuh-tay-fee-YOT.

954. A sweater.

סְוֶדֶר.

suh-VAY-der.

955. A pair of trousers.

זוּג מִכְנָסַיִם.

zoog meekh-na-SAH-yeem.

956. Undershirts.

גּוּפִיּוֹת.

goo-fee-YOT.

BOOKSHOP AND STATIONERY
חֲנוּת סְפָרִים וּכְלֵי כְּתִיבָה

957. Where is there [a bookshop]?

אֵיפֹה יֵשׁ [חֲנוּת סְפָרִים]?

ay-FOH yesh [kha-NOOT sfa-REEM]?

958. —— a stationery.

חֲנוּת כְּלֵי כְּתִיבָה.

kha-NOOT klay ktee-VAH.

959. —— a newsdealer.

מוֹכֵר עִתּוֹנִים.

mo-KHAYR ee-to-NEEM.

960. I want to buy [a book].

אֲבַקֵּשׁ לִקְנוֹת [סֵפֶר].

a-va-KAYSH leek-NOT [SAY-fehr].

961. —— a guidebook.

מַדְרִיךְ.

mad-REEKH.

962. —— a blotter.

נְיַר סוֹפֵג.

nyahr so-FAYG.

963. —— an assortment of picture postcards.

סְדָרָה שֶׁל גְּלוּיוֹת מַרְאֶה.

seed-RAH shel gloo-YOT mar-EH.

964. —— a deck of playing cards.

חֲבִילַת קְלָפִים.

kha-vee-LAT kla-FEEM.

965. —— a dictionary.

מִלּוֹן.

mee-LON.

966. – —— one dozen envelopes.

תְּרֵיסַר מַעֲטָפוֹת.

tray-SAHR ma-a-ta-FOT.

967. —— an eraser.
מֹחַק.
mo-KHAYK.

968. —— ink.
דְּיוֹ.
dyo.

969. —— some magazines.
כַּמָּה יַרְחוֹנִים.
ka-MAH yar-kho-NEEM.

970. —— a map of ——.
מַפַּת ——.
ma-PAT ——.

971. —— some artist's materials.
חָמְרֵי אֻמָּנוּת.
khom-RAY o-ma-NOOT.

972. —— a newspaper.
עִתּוֹן.
ee-TON.

973. —— carbon paper.
נְיָר פֶּחָם.
nyahr peh-KHAM.

974. —— a sheet of wrapping paper.
גִּלְיוֹן נְיָר אֲרִיזָה.
geel-YON nyahr a-ree-ZAH.

975. —— writing paper.
נְיָר מִכְתָּבִים.
nyahr meekh-ta-VEEM.

976. —— a ream of typing paper.

חֲבִילַת נְיָר כְּתִיבָה.

kha-vee-LAT nyahr ktee-VAH.

977. —— a typewriter ribbon.

סֶרֶט לִמְכוֹנַת כְּתִיבָה.

SEH-ret leem-kho-NAT ktee-VAH.

978. —— a fountain pen.

עֵט נוֹבֵעַ.

et no-VAY-a.

979. —— a pencil.

עִפָּרוֹן.

ee-pa-RON.

980. —— string.

חֶבֶל.

KHEH-vel.

981. —— a roll of gummed tape.

גְּלִיל נְיָר דֶּבֶק.

gleel nyahr DEH-vek.

PHOTOGRAPHY

צִלּוּם·

982. I want a roll of movie film for this camera.

אֲבַקֵּשׁ גְּלִיל סֶרֶט הַסְרָטָה עֲבוּר צַלְמוֹנִיָּה זוֹ.

a-va-KAYSH gleel SEH-ret has-ra-TAH a-VOOR tsal-mo-nee-YAH zoo.

983. Do you have [color film] flashbulbs?

הֲיֵשׁ לָכֶם [פִילְם צִבְעוֹנִי] נוּרִיּוֹת צִלּוּם?

ha-YESH la-khem [feelm tseev-o-NEE] noo-ree-YOT tsee-LOOM?

984. The size is ——.

הַגֹּדֶל הוּא ——.

ha-GO-del hoo ——.

985. What is the charge for [developing a roll]?

כַּמָּה יַעֲלֶה [פִּתּוּחַ גָּלִיל אֶחָד]?

ka-MAH ya-a-LEH [pee-TOO-akh ga-LEEL eh-KHAD]?

986. —— an enlargement.

הַגְדָּלָה.

hag-da-LAH.

987. —— one print of each.

הַדְפָּסָה אַחַת מִכָּל אֶחָד.

had-pa-SAH a-KHAT mee-KOOL eh-KHAD.

988. Please have this ready for me as soon as possible.

נָא לְהָכִין לִי זֹאת בְּהֶקְדֵּם הָאֶפְשָׁרִי.

nah luh-ha-KHEEN lee zot buh-hek-DAYM ha-ef-sha-REE.

BARBER SHOP AND BEAUTY SALON

סַפָּר וּמִסְפָּרָה

989. Where will I find [a good barber]?

אֵיפֹה אֶמְצָא [סַפָּר טוֹב]?

ay-FOH em-TSA [seh-PAHR tov]?

990. —— a beauty parlor.

מִסְפָּרָה.

mees-pa-RAH.

991. I want [a haircut].

אֲבַקֵּשׁ [לְהִסְתַּפֵּר].

a-va-KAYSH [luh-hees-ta-PAYR].

992. —— a facial.

טִפּוּל פָּנִים.

tee-POOL pa-NEEM.

993. —— a massage.

מַסַז'.

ma-SAHJ.

994. —— a hair set.

סִלְסוּל.

seel-SOOL.

995. —— a hair tint.

צְבּוּעַ.

tsee-BOO-a

996. —— a manicure.

מַנִיקוּר.

ma-ree-KOOR.

997. —— a permanent wave.

סִלְסוּל תְּמִידִי.

seel-SOOL. tmee-DEE.

998. —— a shoe shine.

צִחְצוּחַ נַעֲלַיִם.

tsekh-TSOO-akh nah-a-LAH-yeem.

999. Can it be done now?

הַאִם אֶפְשָׁר לַעֲשׂוֹת זֹאת עַכְשָׁיו?

ha-EEM ef-SHAHR la-a-SOT zot akh-SHAHV?

1000. Can I make an appointment for tomorrow?

הַאוּכַל לִקְבּוֹעַ זְמַן לְמָחָר?

ha-oo-KHAL leek-BO-a zman luh-ma-KHAR?

1001. My part is [on this side].

הַשְׁבִיל שֶׁלִּי [בְּצַד זֶה].

ha-SHVEEL sheh-LEE [buh-TSAD zeh].

1002. —— on the other side.

בַּצַד הָאַחֵר.

ba-TSAD ha-a-KHAYR.

1003. —— in the middle.

בָּאֶמְצַע.

ba-EM-tsa.

1004. Do not cut any off the top.

נָא לֹא לִגְזֹז שׁוּם דָּבָר לְמַעְלָה.

nah loh leeg-ZOZ shoom da-VAHR luh-MAH-a-la.

1005. Not too short.

לֹא קָצָר מִדַּי.

loh ka-TSAHR mee-DIE.

1006. Thin it out a little.

(תּוֹצִיא) (תּוֹצִיאִי) קְצָת.

(to-TSEE, TO M.) (to-TSEE-ee, TO F.) kuh-TSAT.

1007. Do not put on hair tonic.

אַל (תָּשִׂים) (תָּשִׂימִי) מֵי שֵׂעָר.

al (ta-SEEM, TO M.) (ta-SEE-mee, TO F.) may-say-AHR.

LAUNDRY AND DRY CLEANING

מַכְבֵּסָה וְנִקּוּי חִימִי

1008. Does [this laundry] give one-day service?

הַאִם [מַכְבֵּסָה זוֹ] מַחֲזִירָה בְּאוֹתוֹ יוֹם?

ha-EEM [makh-bay-SAH zoo] ma-kha-zee-RAH buh-o-TOH yom?

1009. —— this dry cleaner.

מְנַקֶּה חִימִי זֶה.

muh-na-KAY KHEE-mee zeh.

1010. Can I have some laundry done?

הַאוּכַל לָתֵת מַשֶּׁהוּ לְכַבֵּס?

ha-oo-KHAL la-TAYT MAH-sheh-hoo luh-kha-BAYS?

1011. Please wash and mend this shirt.

אֲבַקֵּשׁ לְכַבֵּס וּלְתַקֵּן כֻּתֹּנֶת זוֹ.

a-va-KAYSH luh-kha-BAYS oo-luh-ta-KAYN koo TO-net zoo.

1012. This must not be washed in hot water.

אֶת זֶה אָסוּר לְכַבֵּס בְּמַיִם חַמִּים.

et zeh a-SOOR luh-kha-BAYS buh-MAH-yeem kha-MEEM.

1013. Lukewarm water should be used.

יֵשׁ לְהִשְׁתַּמֵּשׁ בְּמַיִם פּוֹשְׁרִים.

yesh luh-heesh-ta-MAYSH buh-MAH-yeem posh-REEM.

1014. Remove this stain, please.

אֲבַקֵּשׁ לְנַקּוֹת אֶת הַכֶּתֶם הַזֶּה.

a-va-KAYSH luh-na-KOT et ha-KEH-tem ha-zeh.

1015. Do not starch the collar.

אַל (תָּשִׂימִי) עֲמִילָן בַּצַּוָּארוֹן.

al (ta-SEE-mee, TO F.) a-mee-LAN ba-tsa-va-RON.

1016. I want this suit cleaned and pressed.

אֲבַקֵּשׁ לְנַקּוֹת וּלְגַהֵץ חֲלִיפָה זוֹ.

a-va-KAYSH luh-na-KOT oo-luh-ga-HAYTS kha-lee-FAH zoo.

1017. The pocket is torn.

הַכִּיס קָרוּעַ.

ha-KEES ka-ROO-a.

1018. The belt is missing.

חָסְרָה הַחֲגוֹרָה.

kha-say-RAH ha-kha-go-RAH.

1019. Will you sew on the buttons for me?

(הֲתוּכְלִי) לִתְפּוֹר לִי אֶת הַכַּפְתּוֹרִים?

(ha-tookh-LEE, TO F.) leet-POR lee et ha-kaf-to-REEM?

1020. Replace the zipper, please.

אֲבַקֵּשׁ לְהַחֲלִיף אֶת הָרוֹכְסָן.

a-va-KAYSH luh-ha-kha-LEEF et ha-rookh-SAN.

REPAIRS

תִּקּוּנִים

1021. My glasses are broken.

הַמִּשְׁקָפַיִם שֶׁלִּי שְׁבוּרוֹת.

lu-meesh-ka-FAH-yeem sheh-LEE shvoo-ROT.

1022. Please regulate my watch.

נָא לְכַוֵּן אֶת הַשָּׁעוֹן שֶׁלִּי.

nah luh-kha-VAYN et ha-sha-ON sheh-LEE.

1023. My clock [loses] gains time.

הַשָּׁעוֹן שֶׁלִּי [מְפַגֵּר] מְמַהֵר.

ha-sha-ON sheh-LEE [muh-fa-GAYR] muh-ma-HAYR.

1024. My hearing aid does not function well.

מַכְשִׁיר הַשְּׁמִיעָה שֶׁלִּי לֹא פּוֹעֵל בְּסֵדֶר.

makh-SHEER hash-mee-AH sheh-LEE loh po-AYL buh-SEH-dehr.

1025. Please repair [the sole].

אֲבַקֵּשׁ לְתַקֵּן [אֶת הַסֻּלְיָה].

a-va-KAYSH luh-ta-KAYN [et ha-sool-YAH].

1026. —— the heel.

הֶעָקֵב.

heh-a-KAYV.

1027. —— the uppers.

הָעוֹר הָעֶלְיוֹן.

ha-OR ha-el-YON.

1028. —— the strap.

הָרְצוּעָה.

har-tsoo-AH.

HEALTH AND ILLNESS

בְּרִיאוּת וּמַחֲלָה

1029. I need a doctor.

אֲנִי (צָרִיךְ) (צְרִיכָה) רוֹפֵא.

a-NEE (tsa-REEKH, M.) (tsree-KHAH, F.) ro-FAY.

1030. An American doctor.

רוֹפֵא אֲמֶרִיקָאִי.

ro-FAY a-meh-ree-KAH-ee.

1031. A doctor who speaks English.

רוֹפֵא הַמְּדַבֵּר אַנְגְּלִית.

ro-FAY ha-muh-da-BAYR ang-LEET.

1032. A specialist.

רוֹפֵא מוּמְחֶה.

ro-FAY moom-KHEH.

1033. A chiropodist.

רוֹפֵא רַגְלַיִם.

ro-FAY rag-LAH-yeem.

1034. An oculist.

רוֹפֵא עֵינַיִם.

ro-FAY ay-NAH-yeem.

1035. Is the doctor in?

הַאִם הָרוֹפֵא בַּבַּיִת?

ha-EEM ha-ro-FAY ba-BAH-yeet?

1036. I have something in my eye.

יֵשׁ לִי מַשֶּׁהוּ בָּעַיִן.

yesh lee MAH-shuh-hoo ba-AH-yeen.

1037. I have a headache.

יֵשׁ לִי כְּאֵב רֹאשׁ.

yesh lee kuh-AYV rosh.

1038. I have a pain in my back.*

יֵשׁ לִי כְּאֵב בַּגַּב.

yesh lee kuh-AYV ba-GAV.

1039. I do not sleep well.

אֵינֶנִּי (יָשֵׁן) (יְשֵׁנָה) טוֹב.

ay-NEH-nee (ya-SHAYN, m.) (yuh-shay-NAH, f.)
tov.

1040. Can you give me something to relieve my allergy?

(הֲתוּכַל) לָתֵת לִי מַשֶּׁהוּ נֶגֶד הָאַלֶרְגִּיָה שֶׁלִּי?

(ha-too-KHAL, TO M.) la-TAYT lee MAH-shuh-hoo
NEH-ged ha-a-LEHR-gya sheh-LEE?

* For a complete list of PARTS OF THE BODY, see p. 148.

1041. An appendicitis attack.

הִתְקָפַת הַמְּעִי הָעִוֵּר.

hat-ka-FAT ha-muh-EE ha-ee-VAYR.

1042. A mosquito bite.

עֲקִיצַת יַתּוּשׁ.

a-kee-TSAT ya-TOOSH.

1043. A blister.

אֲבַעְבּוּעָה.

a-vah-a-boo-AH.

1044. A boil.

מוּרְסָה.

moor-SAH.

1045. A burn.

כְּוִיָה.

kvee-YAH.

1046. Chills.

צְמַרְמֹרֶת.

tsmar-MO-ret.

1047. A cold.

הִצְטַנְּנוּת.

heets-ta-nuh-NOOT.

1048. Constipation.

עֲצִירוּת.

a-tsee-ROOT.

1049. A cough.

שָׁעוּל.

shee-OOL.

1050. A cramp.

הִתְכַּוְּצוּת.

heet-kav-TSOOT.

1051. Diarrhoea.

שִׁלְשׁוּל.

sheel-SHOOL.

1052. Dysentery.

דִּיסֶנְטֶרְיָה.

dee-sen-TEHR-ya.

1053. An earache.

כְּאֵב אָזְנַיִם.

kuh-AYV oz-NAH-yeem.

1054. A fever.

חֹם.

khom.

1055. Hoarseness.

צְרִידוּת.

tsree-DOOT.

1056. Indigestion.

קִלְקוּל הַקֵּבָה.

keel-KOOL ha-kay-VAH.

1057. An infection.

הִדַּבְקוּת.

hee-dab-KOOT.

1058. Nausea.

בְּחִילָה.

buh-khee-LAH.

1059. Pneumonia.

דַּלֶּקֶת רֵאוֹת.

da-LEH-ket ray-OT.

1060. A sore throat.

כְּאֵב גָּרוֹן.

kuh-AYV ga-RON.

1061. A sunburn.

כְּוִיַת שֶׁמֶשׁ.

kvee-YAT SHEH-mesh.

1062. A virus.

וִירוּס.

VEE-roos.

1063. What shall I do?

מֶה עָלַי לַעֲשׂוֹת?

meh a-LIE la-a-SOT?

1064. Do I have to go to a hospital?

הַאִם עָלַי לָלֶכֶת לְבֵית חוֹלִים?

ha-EEM a-LIE la-LEH-khet luh-VAYT kho-LEEM?

1065. Must I stay in bed?

הַאִם עָלַי לְהִשָּׁאֵר בַּמִּטָּה?

ha-EEM a-LIE luh-hee-sha-AYR ba-mee-TAH?

1066. Is it contagious?

הַאִם זֶה מִדַּבֵּק?

ha-EEM zeh muh-da-BAYK?

1067. I feel [better] worse.

אֲנִי מַרְגִּישׁ יוֹתֵר [טוֹב] רָע.

a-NEE mar-GEESH yoh-TAYR [tohv] ra.

1068. Can I travel on Monday?

הַאוּכַל לִנְסוֹעַ בְּיוֹם שֵׁנִי?

ha-oo-KHAL leen-SO-a buh-yom shay-NEE?

1069. When will you come again?

(מָתַי תָּבֹא) עוֹד פַּעַם?

(ma-TIE ta-VO, то м.) od PA-am?

1070. When shall I take [the medicine]?

מָתַי עָלַי לָקַחַת אֶת [הָרְפוּאָה]?

ma-TIE a-LIE la-KA-khat et [har-foo-AH]?

1071. ——— the pills.

הַכַּדּוּרִים.

ha-ka-doo-REEM.

1072. Every hour.

כָּל שָׁעָה.

kol sha-AH.

1073. [Before] after meals.

[לִפְנֵי] אַחֲרֵי הָאֲרוּחוֹת.

[leef-NAY] a-kha-RAY ha-a-roo-KHOT.

1074. On going to bed.

לִפְנֵי הַשֵּׁנָה.

leef-NAY ha-shay-NAH.

1075. On getting up.

כְּשֶׁקָּמִים.

kuh-shuh-ka-MEEM.

1076. Twice a day.

פַּעֲמַיִם בַּיּוֹם.

pa-a-MAH-yeem ba-YOM.

1077. A drop.

טִפָּה.

tee-PAH.

1078. A teaspoonful.

כַּפִּית.

ka-PEET.

1079. X-rays.

שִׁקּוּף.

shee-KOOF.

ACCIDENTS

תְּאוּנוֹת

1080. There has been an accident.

הָיְתָה תְּאוּנָה.

hie-TAH tuh-oo-NAH.

1081. Please call [a doctor].

נָא לִקְרֹא [לְרוֹפֵא].

nah leek-RO [tuh-ro-FAY].

1082. —— a nurse.

אָחוֹת.

a-KHOT.

1083. —— an ambulance.

אַמְבּוּלַנְס.

am-boo-LANS.

1084. He has [fallen] fainted.

הוּא [נָפַל] הִתְעַלֵף:

hoo [na-FAL] heet-a-LAYF.

1085. She has [a bruise].

הִיא קִבְּלָה [מַכָּה].

hee keeb-LAH [ma-KAH].

1086. —— a cut.

חָתָךְ.

kha-TAKH.

1087. —— a fracture.

שֶׁבֶר.

SHEH-vehr.

1088. —— a sprain.

נֶקַע.

NEH-ka.

1089. Can you dress this wound?

הַאִם (אַתָּה יָכֹל) (אַתְּ יְכוֹלָה) לַחֲבוֹשׁ אֶת הַפֶּצַע הַזֶּה?

ha-EEM (a-TAH ya-KHOL, TO M.) (at yuh-khu-LAH, TO F.) la-kha-VOSH et ha-PEH-tsa ha-ZEH?

1090. It is bleeding.

יוֹרֵד דָם.

yo-RAYD dam.

1091. It is swollen.

זֶה נָפוּחַ.

zeh na-FOO-akh.

1092. I need something for a tourniquet.

נָחוּץ לִי מַשֶּׁהוּ לַעֲצוֹר אֶת הַדָּם.

na-KHOOTS lee MAH-shuh-hoo la-a-TSOR et ha-DAM.

1093. Are you all right?

הַאִם (אַתָּה מַרְגִּישׁ) (אַתְּ מַרְגִּישָׁה) בְּסֵדֶר?

ha-EEM (a-TAH mar-GEESH, TO M.) (at mar-gee-SHAH, TO F.) buh-SEH-dehr?

1094. I have hurt my foot.

פָּצַעְתִּי אֶת הָרֶגֶל שֶׁלִּי.

pah-TSA-tee et ha-REH-gel sheh-LEE.

1095. I want to rest for a moment.

אֲנִי (רוֹצֶה) (רוֹצָה) לָנוּחַ לְרֶגַע.

a-NEE (ro-TSEH, M.) (ro-TSAH, F.) la-NOO-akh luh-REH-ga.

1096. Please notify [my husband].

נָא לְהוֹדִיעַ [לְבַעֲלִי].

nah luh-ho-DEE-a [luh-va-a-LEE].

1097. —— my wife.

לְאִשְׁתִּי.

luh-eesh-TEE.

1098. —— my friend.

(לַחֲבֵרִי) (לְחֲבֵרְתִּי).

(la-kha-vay-REE, M.) (luh-kha-vayr-TEE, F.).

PARTS OF THE BODY

אֶבְרֵי הַגּוּף

1099. The appendix.

הַמְּעִי הָעִוֵּר.

ha-muh-EE ha-ee-VAYR.

1100. The arm.
הַזְּרוֹעַ.
ha-ZRO-a.

1101. The artery.
הָעֹרֶק.
ha-O-rek.

1102. The back.
הַגַּב.
ha-GAV.

1103. The blood.
הַדָּם.
ha-DAM.

1104. The blood vessels.
צִנּוֹרוֹת הַדָּם.
tsee-noh-ROT ha-DAM.

1105. The bone.
הָעֶצֶם.
ha-EH-tsem.

1106. The brain.
הַמֹּוחַ.
ha-MO-akh.

1107. The breast.
הַשַּׁד.
ha-SHAD.

1108. The cheek.
הַלֶּחִי.
ha-LEH-khee.

1109. The chest.

הֶחָזֶה.

heh-kha-ZEH.

1110. The chin.

הַסַּנְטֵר.

ha-san-TAYR.

1111. The collarbone.

עֶצֶם הַצַּוָּאר.

EH-tsem ha-tsa-VAHR.

1112. The ear.

הָאֹזֶן.

ha-O-zen.

1113. The elbow.

הַמַּרְפֵּק.

ha-mar-PAYK.

1114. The eye.

הָעַיִן.

ha-AH-yeen.

1115. The eyebrows.

הַגַּבּוֹת.

ha-ga-BOT.

1116. The eyelashes.

הָרִיסִים.

ha-ree-SEEM.

1117. The eyelid.

הָעַפְעַף.

ha-af-AF.

1118. The face.

הַפָּנִים.

ha-pa-NEEM.

1119. The finger.

הָאֶצְבַּע.

ha-ETS-ba.

1120. The fingernail.

צִפֹּרֶן הָאֶצְבַּע.

tsee-PO-ren ha-ETS-ba.

1121. The foot.

הָרֶגֶל.

ha-REH-gel.

1122. The forehead.

הַמֵּצַח.

ha-MEH-tsakh.

1123. The gall bladder.

שַׁלְפּוּחִית הַמָּרָה.

shal-poo-KHEET ha-ma-RAH.

1124. The glands.

הַבַּלוּטוֹת.

ha-ba-loo-TOT.

1125. The gums.

הַחֲנִיכַיִם.

ha-kha-nee-KHAH-yeem.

1126. The hair.

הַשֵּׂעָר.

ha-say-AHR.

1127. The head.
הָרֹאשׁ.
ha-ROSH.

1128. The hand.
הַיָּד.
ha-YAD.

1129. The heart.
הַלֵּב.
ha-LAYV.

1130. The heel.
הֶעָקֵב.
heh-a-KAYV.

1131. The hip.
הַמֹּתֶן.
ha-MO-ten.

1132. The intestines.
הַמֵּעַיִם.
ha-may-AH-yeem.

1133. The jaw.
הַלֶּסֶת.
ha-LEH-set.

1134. The joint.
הַפֶּרֶק.
ha-PEH-rek.

1135. The kidney.
הַכִּלְיָה.
hak-la-YAH.

1136. The leg.
הָרֶגֶל.
ha-REH-gel.

1137. The lip.
הַשָּׂפָה.
ha-sa-FAH.

1138. The liver.
הַכָּבֵד.
ha-ka-VAYD.

1139. The lung.
הָרֵאָה.
ha-ray-AH.

1140. The mouth.
הַפֶּה.
ha-PEH.

1141. The muscle.
הַשָּׁרִיר.
ha-sha-REER.

1142. The neck.
הַצַּוָּאר.
ha-tsa-VAHR.

1143. The nerve.
הָעֶצֶב.
ha-EH-tsev.

1144. The nose.
הָאַף.
ha-AF.

1145. The rib.
הַצֵּלָע.
ha-TSEH-la.

1146. The shoulder.
הַכָּתֵף.
ha-ka-TAYF.

1147. The skin.
הָעוֹר.
ha-OR.

1148. The skull.
הַקָּדְקֹד.
ha-kod-KOD.

1149. The spine.
חוּט הַשִּׁדְרָה.
khoot ha-shed-RAH.

1150. The stomach.
הַקֵּבָה.
ha-kay-VAH.

1151. The teeth.
הַשִּׁנַּיִם.
ha-shee-NAH-yeem.

1152. The toe.
אֶצְבַּע הָרֶגֶל.
ETS-ba ha-REH-gel.

1153. The toenail.
צִפֹּרֶן אֶצְבַּע הָרֶגֶל.
tsee-PO-ren ETS-ba ha-REH-gel.

1154. The tongue.

הַלָשׁוֹן.

ha-la-SHON.

1155. The tonsils.

הַשְׁקֵדִים.

hash-kay-DEEM.

1156. The vein.

הַוָרִיד.

ha-va-REED.

1157. The wrist.

פֶּרֶק הַיָד.

PEH-rek ha-YAD.

DENTIST

רוֹפֵא שִׁנַּיִם

1158. Do you know a good dentist?

הַאִם (אַתָּה יוֹדֵעַ) (אַתְּ יוֹדַעַת) עַל רוֹפֵא שִׁנַּיִם
טוֹב?

*ha-EEM (a-TAH yo-DAY-a, TO M.) (at yo-DAH-at
TO F.), al ro-FAY shee-NAH-yeem tov?*

1159. I have lost a filling.

יָצְאָה לִי סְתִימָה.

yats-AH lee stee-MAH.

1160. This wisdom tooth hurts me.

שֵׁן בִּינָה זוּ כּוֹאֶבֶת לִי.

shayn bee-NAH zoo ko-EH-vet lee.

1161. I think I have [an abscess] a broken tooth.

חוֹשְׁבַנִי שֶׁיֵּשׁ לִי [מוּרְסָה] שֵׁן שְׁבוּרָה.

khosh-VAH-nee shuh-YESH lee [moor-SAH] shayn shvoo-RAH.

1162. Can you fix the bridge temporarily?

(הַתּוּכַל לְסַדֵּר אֶת הַגֶּשֶׁר בְּאֹפֶן זְמַנִּי

(ha-too-KHAL, TO M.) luh-sa-DAYR et ha-GEH-shehr buh-o-FAN zma-NEE?

1163. The denture.

הַשִּׁנַּיִם הַתּוֹתָבוֹת.

ha-shee-NAH-yeem ha-to-ta-VOT.

1164. This is hurting me.

זֶה כּוֹאֵב לִי.

zeh ko-AYV lee.

1165. Please give me [a local anesthetic] gas.

אֲבַקֵּשׁ לָתֵת לִי [אַנֶסְטֶזְיָה מְקוֹמִית] גַּז.

a-va-KAYSH la-TAYT lee [a-nes-TAYZ-yah muh-ko-MEET] gas.

USEFUL INFORMATION: TIME

שׁוֹנוֹת: זְמַן

1166. What time is it?

מַה הַשָּׁעָה?

mah ha-sha-AH?

1167. It is [early].

זֶה [מוּקְדָּם].

zeh [mook-DAM].

1168. —— too late.

מְאוּחָר מִדַּי.

muh-oo-KHAHR mee-DIE.

1169. —— two o'clock A.M.

שְׁתַּיִם בַּבֹּקֶר.

SHTAH-yeem ba-BO-kehr.

1170. —— half-past three P.M.

שָׁלֹשׁ וָחֵצִי אַחֲרֵי הַצָּהֳרַיִם.

sha-LOSH va-KHAY-tsee a-kha-RAY ha-tso-ha-RAH-yeem.

1171. —— quarter-past four.

אַרְבַּע וָרֶבַע.

ar-BA va-REH-va.

1172. —— quarter to five.

רֶבַע לְחָמֵשׁ.

REH-va luh-kha-MAYSH.

1173. At ten minutes to six.

בְּשֵׁשׁ פָּחוֹת עֲשָׂרָה.

buh-SHAYSH pa-KHOT a-sa-RAH.

1174. At twelve minutes past seven.

בְּשֶׁבַע וּשְׁנַיִם־עָשָׂר.

buh-SHEH-va oo-SHNAYM-a-sahr.

1175. In the morning.

בַּבֹּקֶר.

ba-BO-kehr.

1176. In the afternoon.

אַחֲרֵי הַצָּהֳרַיִם.

a-kha-RAY ha-tso-ha-RAH-yeem.

1177. In the evening.

בָּעֶרֶב.

ba-EH-rev.

1178. At noon.

בַּצָּהֳרַיִם.

ba-tso-ha-RAH-yeem.

1179. The day.

הַיּוֹם.

ha-YOM.

1180. The night.

הַלַּיְלָה.

ha-LIE-la.

1181. Midnight.

חֲצוֹת.

kha-TSOT.

1182. Last night.

אֶמֶשׁ.

EH-mesh.

1183. Yesterday.

אֶתְמוֹל.

et-MOL.

1184. Today.

הַיּוֹם.

ha-YOM.

1185. Tonight.

הָעֶרֶב.

ha-EH-rev.

1186. Tomorrow.

מָחָר.

ma-KHAR.

1187. Last month.

בַּחֹדֶשׁ שֶׁעָבַר.

ba-KHO-desh sheh-a-VAR.

1188. Last year.

אֶשְׁתָּקַד.

esh-ta-KEHD.

1189. Next week.

בַּשָּׁבוּעַ הַבָּא.

ba-sha-VOO-a ha-BA.

1190. Next Sunday.

בְּיוֹם רִאשׁוֹן הַבָּא.

buh-yom ree-SHON ha-BA.

1191. The day before yesterday.

שִׁלְשׁוֹם.

sheel-SHOM.

1192. The day after tomorrow.

מָחֳרָתַיִם.

mokh-ro-TAH-yeem.

1193. Two weeks ago.

לִפְנֵי שָׁבוּעַיִם.

leef-NAY shvoo-AH-yeem.

WEATHER

מֶזֶג הָאֲוִיר

1194. How is the weather today?

אֵיךְ מֶזֶג הָאֲוִיר הַיּוֹם?

aykh MEH-zeg ha-a-VEER ha-YOM?

1195. Is it [cold]?

הַאִם [קַר]?

ha-EEM [kar]?

1196. —— fair.

נָעִים.

na-EEM.

1197. —— hot.

חַם.

kham.

1198. —— raining.

יוֹרֵד גֶּשֶׁם.

yo-RAYD GEH-shem.

1199. —— snowing.

יוֹרֵד שֶׁלֶג.

yo-RAYD SHEH-leg.

1200. —— sunny.

הַשֶּׁמֶשׁ זוֹרַחַת.

ha-SHEH-mesh zo-RA-khat.

1201. —— very warm.

חַם מְאֹד.

kham muh-OD.

1202. I want to sit in the shade.

אֲנִי (רוֹצֶה) (רוֹצָה) לָשֶׁבֶת בַּצֵּל.

a-NEE (ro-TSEH, M) (ro-TSAH, F.) la-SHEH-vet ba-TSAYL.

1203. In the sun.

בַּשֶּׁמֶשׁ.

ba-SHEH-mesh.

DAYS OF THE WEEK

יְמֵי הַשָּׁבוּעַ

1204. Monday.

יוֹם שֵׁנִי.

yom shay-NEE.

1205. Tuesday.

יוֹם שְׁלִישִׁי.

yom shlee-SHEE.

1206. Wednesday.

יוֹם רְבִיעִי.

yom ruh-vee-EE.

1207. Thursday.

יוֹם חֲמִישִׁי.

yom kha-mee-SHEE.

1208. Friday.

יוֹם שִׁשִּׁי.

yom shee-SHEE.

1209. Saturday.

שַׁבָּת.

sha-BAT.

1210. Sunday.

יוֹם רִאשׁוֹן.

yom ree-SHON.

MONTHS AND SEASONS

חֳדָשִׁים וְעוֹנוֹת

1211. January.

יַנּוּאַר.

YA-noo-ar.

1212. February.

פֶּבְּרוּאַר.

FEB-roo-ar.

1213. March.

מַרְס.

mars.

1214. April.

אַפְּרִיל.

ap-REEL.

1215. May.

מַאי.

mie.

1216. June.

יוּנִי.

YOO-nee.

1217. July.

יוּלִי.

YOO-lee.

1218. August.

אוֹגוּסְט.

o-GOOST.

1219. September.

סֶפְּטֶמְבֶּר.

sep-TEM-behr.

1220. October.

אוֹקְטוֹבֶּר.

ok-TO-behr.

1221. November.

נוֹבֶמְבֶּר.

no-VEM-behr.

1222. December.

דֶּצֶמְבֶּר.

deh-TSEM-behr.

1223. Spring.

אָבִיב.

a-VEEV.

1224. Summer.

קַיִץ.

KAH-yeets.

1225. Autumn.

סְתָיו.

stav.

1226. Winter.

חֹרֶף.

KHO-ref.

HOLIDAYS AND GREETINGS
חַגִּים וְאָחוּלִים

1227. Christmas.

חַג הַמּוֹלָד.

khag ha-mo-LAD.

1228. Passover.

פֶּסַח.

PEH-sakh.

1229. Feast of the Tabernacles.

סֻכּוֹת.

soo-KOT.

1230. Hanukka.

חֲנֻכָּה.

kha-noo-KAH.

1231. New Year.

רֹאשׁ הַשָּׁנָה.

rosh ha-sha-NAH.

1232. Day of Atonement.

יוֹם כִּפּוּר.

yom kee-POOR.

1233. Happy New Year.

שָׁנָה טוֹבָה.

sha-NAH to-VAH.

1234. Happy holiday.

חַג שָׂמֵחַ *or* מוֹעֲדִים לְשִׂמְחָה.

khag so-MAY-akh or mo-a-DEEM luh-seem-KHAH.

1235. All the best.

כָּל טוּב.

kol toov.

1236. Congratulations.

מַזָּל טוֹב.

ma-ZAL tov.

NUMBERS

מִסְפָּרִים

(NOTE: The first form given is *masc.*, the second—*fem.*
When only one form appears, it can be used for
both *m.* and *f.* forms.)

1237. One.

אֶחָד, אַחַת.

eh-KHAD, a-KHAT.

Two.

שְׁנַיִם, שְׁתַּיִם.

SHNAH-yeem, SHTAH-yeem.

Three.

שְׁלֹשָׁה, שָׁלֹשׁ.

shlo-SHAH, sha-LOSH.

Four.

אַרְבָּעָה, אַרְבַּע.

ar-ba-AH, ar-BAH.

Five.

חֲמִשָּׁה, חָמֵשׁ.

kha-mee-SHAH, kha-MAYSH.

Six.

שִׁשָּׁה, שֵׁשׁ.

shee-SHAH, shaysh.

Seven.

שִׁבְעָה, שֶׁבַע.

sheev-AH, SHEH-va.

Eight.

שְׁמֹנָה, שְׁמֹנֶה.

shmo-NAH, SHMO-neh.

Nine.

תִּשְׁעָה, תֵּשַׁע.

teesh-AH, TAY-sha.

Ten.

עֲשָׂרָה, עֶשֶׂר.

a-sa-RAH, EH-sehr.

Eleven.

אַחַד־עָשָׂר, אַחַת־עֶשְׂרֵה.

a-KHAD-a-SAHR, a-KHAT-es-RAY.

Twelve.

שְׁנַיִם־עָשָׂר, שְׁתַּיִם־עֶשְׂרֵה.

SHNAYM-a-SAHR, SHTAYM-es-RAY.

Thirteen.

שְׁלֹשָׁה־עָשָׂר, שְׁלֹשׁ־עֶשְׂרֵה.

shlo-SHAH-a-SAHR, SHLOSH-es-RAY.

Fourteen.

אַרְבָּעָה־עָשָׂר, אַרְבַּע־עֶשְׂרֵה.

ar-ba-AH-a-SAHR, ar-BAH-es-RAY.

Fifteen.

חֲמִשָּׁה־עָשָׂר, חֲמֵשׁ־עֶשְׂרֵה.

kha-mee-SHAH-a-SAHR, kha-MAYSH-es-RAY.

Sixteen.

שִׁשָּׁה־עָשָׂר, שֵׁשׁ־עֶשְׂרֵה.

shee-SHAH-a-SAHR, SHAYSH-es-RAY.

Seventeen.

שִׁבְעָה־עָשָׂר, שְׁבַע־עֶשְׂרֵה.

sheev-AH-a-SAHR, SHVAH-es-RAY.

Eighteen.

שְׁמֹנָה־עָשָׂר, שְׁמֹנֶה־עֶשְׂרֵה.

shmo-NAH-a-SAHR, shmo-NEH-es-RAY.

Nineteen.

תִּשְׁעָה־עָשָׂר, תְּשַׁע־עֶשְׂרֵה.

teesh-AH-a-SAHR, TSHAH-es-RAY.

Twenty.

עֶשְׂרִים.

es-REEM.

Twenty-one.

עֶשְׂרִים־וְאֶחָד, עֶשְׂרִים־וְאַחַת.

es-REEM-vuh-eh-KHAD, es-REEM-vuh-a-KHAT.

Twenty-two.

עֶשְׂרִים־וּשְׁנַיִם, עֶשְׂרִים־וּשְׁתַּיִם.

es-REEM-vuh-SHNAH-yeem, es-REEM-vuh-SHTAH-yeem.

Thirty.

שְׁלֹשִׁים.

shlo-SHEEM.

Thirty-one.

שְׁלֹשִׁים־וְאֶחָד, שְׁלֹשִׁים־וְאַחַת.

shlo-SHEEM-vuh-eh-KHAD,   shlo-SHEEM-vah-a-
KHAT.

Forty.

אַרְבָּעִים.

ar-ba-EEM.

Fifty.

חֲמִשִּׁים.

kha-mee-SHEEM.

Sixty.

שִׁשִּׁים.

shee-SHEEM.

Seventy.

שִׁבְעִים.

sheev-EEM.

Seventy-one.

שִׁבְעִים־וְאֶחָד, שִׁבְעִים־וְאַחַת.

sheev-EEM-vuh-eh-KHAD, sheev-EEM-vuh-a-
KHAT.

Eighty.

שְׁמֹנִים.

shmo-NEEM.

Eighty-one.

שְׁמֹנִים־וְאֶחָד, שְׁמֹנִים־וְאַחַת.

shmo-NEEM-vuh-eh-KHAD, shmo-NEEM-vuh-a
KHAT.

Ninety.

תִּשְׁעִים.

teesh-EEM.

Ninety-one.

תִּשְׁעִים־וְאֶחָד, תִּשְׁעִים־וְאַחַת.

teesh-EEM-vuh-eh-KHAD, teesh-EEM-vuh-a-KHAT.

One hundred.

מֵאָה.

meh-AH.

Two hundred.

מָאתַיִם.

ma-TAH-yeem.

One thousand.

אֶלֶף.

EH-lef.

Two thousand.

אַלְפַּיִם.

al-PAH-yeem.

Today's date is ——.

הַתַּאֲרִיךְ שֶׁל הַיּוֹם הוּא ——.

ha-ta-a-REEKH shel ha-YOM hoo ——.

NUMBERS: ORDINALS

מִסְפָּרִים סְדוּרִיִּים

1238. First.

רִאשׁוֹן, רִאשׁוֹנָה.

ree-SHON, ree-sho-NAH.

Second.

שֵׁנִי, שְׁנִיָּה.

shay-NEE, shnee-YAH.

Third.

שְׁלִישִׁי, שְׁלִישִׁית.

shlee-SHEE, shlee-SHEET.

Fourth.

רְבִיעִי, רְבִיעִית.

ruh-vee-EE, ruh-vee-EET.

Fifth.

חֲמִישִׁי, חֲמִישִׁית.

kha-mee-SHEE, kha-mee-SHEET.

Sixth.

שִׁשִּׁי, שִׁשִּׁית.

shee-SHEE, shee-SHEET.

Seventh.

שְׁבִיעִי, שְׁבִיעִית.

shvee-EE, shvee-EET.

Eighth.

שְׁמִינִי, שְׁמִינִית.

shmee-NEE, shmee-NEET.

Ninth.

תְּשִׁיעִי, תְּשִׁיעִית.

tshee-EE, tshee-EET.

Tenth.

עֲשִׂירִי, עֲשִׂירִית.

a-see-REE, a-see-REET.

USEFUL ARTICLES

חֶפְצֵי יוֹם־יוֹם

1239. The ash tray.

הַמַּאֲפֵרָה.

ha-ma-a-fay-RAH.

1240. The basket.

הַסַּל.

ha-SAL.

1241. The bobby pins.

סִכּוֹת הָרֹאשׁ.

see-KOT ha-ROSH.

1242. The bottle opener.

מַפְתֵּחַ הַבַּקְבּוּקִים.

maf-TAY-akh ha-bak-boo-KEEM.

1243. The box.

הַתֵּבָה.

ha-teh-VAH.

1244. The bracelet.

הַצָּמִיד.

ha-tsa-MEED.

1245. The light bulb.

הַנּוּרִית.

ha-noo-REET.

1246. The candy.

הַסֻּכָּרִיָּה.

ha-soo-ka-ree-YAH.

1247. The can opener.

מַפְתֵּחַ הַפָּחִיּוֹת.

maf-TAY-akh ha-pa-khee-YOT.

1248. The china.

הַחַרְסִינָה.

ha-khar-see-NAH.

1249. The cloth.

הַבַּד.

ha-BAD.

1250. The clock.

הַשָּׁעוֹן.

ha-sha-ON.

1251. The compact.

הַפּוּדְרִיָה.

ha-pood-ree-YAH.

1252. The cotton.

הַכֻּתְנָה.

ha-koot-NAH.

1253. The absorbent cotton.

צֶמֶר הַגֶּפֶן.

TSEH-mehr ha-GEH-fen.

1254. The cork.

הַפְּקָק.

ha-puh-KAK.

1255. The corkscrew.

הַמַּחֲלֵץ.

ha-ma-kha-LAYTS.

1256. The cuff links.
כַּפְתּוֹרֵי הַשַּׁרְווּל.
kaf-to-RAY ha-shar-VOOL.

1257. The cushion.
הַכַּר.
ha-KAHR.

1258. The doll.
הַבֻּבָּה
ha-boo-BAH.

1259. The earrings.
הָעֲגִילִים.
ha-a-gee-LEEM.

1260. The embroidery.
הָרִקְמָה.
ha-reek-MAH.

1261. The flashlight.
הַפַּנָּס.
ha-pa-NAS.

1262. The chewing gum.
הַמַּסְתִּיק.
ha-MAS-teek.

1263. The handbag.
הָאַרְנָק.
ha-ar-NAK.

1264. The hairnet.
רֶשֶׁת הַשְּׂעָרוֹת.
REH-shet ha-suh-a-ROT.

1265. The iron (flat).

הַמַּגְהֵץ.

ha-mag-HAYTS.

1266. The jewelry—gold, silver.

הַתַּכְשִׁיטִים—זָהָב, כֶּסֶף.

ha-takh-shee-TEEM—za-HAV, KEH-sef.

1267. The lace.

הַתַּחֲרִים.

ha-takh-REEM.

1268. The leather.

הָעוֹר.

ha-OR.

1269. The linen.

הַפִּשְׁתָּן.

ha-peesh-TAN.

1270. The mirror.

הָרְאִי.

ha-ruh-EE.

1271. The musical instruments.

כְּלֵי הַנְּגִינָה.

klay han-gee-NAH.

1272. The sheet music.

הַתָּוִים.

ha-ta-VEEM.

1273. The mosquito net.

רֶשֶׁת הַיַּתּוּשִׁים.

REH-shet ha-ya-too-SHEEM.

1274. The nail file.
מַבְרֵד הַצִּפָּרְנַיִם.
mav-RAYD ha-tsee-por-NAH-yeem.

1275. The necklace.
הָעֲנָק.
ha-a-NAK.

1276. The needle.
הַמַּחַט.
ha-MA-khat.

1277. The notebook.
הַפִּנְקָס.
ha-peen-KAS.

1278. The oil painting.
צִיּוּר הַשֶּׁמֶן.
tsee-YOOR ha-SHEH-men.

1279. The pail.
הַדְּלִי.
ha-DLEE.

1280. The penknife.
הָאוֹלָר.
ha-o-LAHR.

1281. The perfume.
הַבֹּשֶׂם.
ha-BO-sem.

1282. The pin.
הַסִּכָּה.
ha-see-KAH.

1283. The radio.

הַמַּקְלֵט *or* הָרַדְיוֹ.

ha-mak-LATT or ha-RAD-yo.

1284. The phonograph records.

הַתַּקְלִיטִים.

ha-tak-lee-TEEM.

1285. The ring.

הַטַּבַּעַת.

ha-ta-BAH-at.

1286. The rubbers *or* overshoes.

הַמַּגָּפַיִם.

ha-ma-ga-FAH-yeem.

1287. The rug.

הַשָּׁטִיחַ.

ha-sha-TEE-akh.

1288. The scissors.

הַמִּסְפָּרַיִם.

ha-mees-pa-RAH-yeem.

1289. The screw.

הַבֹּרֶג.

ha-BOH-reg.

1290. The silk.

הַמֶּשִׁי.

ha-MEH-shee.

1291. The silverware.

כְּלֵי הַכֶּסֶף.

klay ha-KEH-sef.

1292. The precious stone.
הָאֶבֶן הַיְקָרָה.
ha-EH-ven ha-yuh-ka-RAH.

1293. The stopper.
הַפְּקָק.
ha-puh-KAK.

1294. The tablecloth.
מַפַּת הַשֻּׁלְחָן.
ma-PAT ha-shool-KHAN.

1295. The thimble.
הָאֶצְבָּעוֹן.
ha-ets-ba-ON.

1296. The thread.
הַחוּט.
ha-KHOOT.

1297. The toys.
הַצַּעֲצוּעִים.
ha-tsa-a-tsoo-EEM.

1298. The umbrella.
הַמִּטְרִיָּה.
ha-meet-ree-YAH.

1299. The vase.
הַצִּנְצֶנֶת.
ha-tseen-TSEH-net.

1300. The whiskbroom.
מַטְאֲטֵא הַיָּד.
ma-ta-TAY ha-YAD.

1301. The wire.

חוּט הַבַּרְזֶל.

khoot ha-bar-ZEL.

1302. The wood.

הָעֵץ.

ha-AYTS.

1303. The wool.

הַצֶּמֶר.

ha-TSEH-mehr.

INDEX

All the sentences, phrases and words in this book are numbered consecutively from 1 to 1303. Numbers in the index refer you to each specific entry. In addition each major section (capitalized) is indexed according to page number in **bold face**. Parts of speech are indicated by the following italic abbreviations: *n.* for noun, *v.* for verb, *adj.* for adjective, *adv.* for adverb, *pron.* for pronoun, *prep.* for preposition. Parentheses are used for word explanations.

LISTEN & LEARN CASSETTES

Complete, practical at-home language learning courses for people with limited study time—specially designed for travelers.

Special features:

• Dual-language—Each phrase first in English, then the foreign-language equivalent, followed by a pause for repetition (allows for easy use of cassette even without manual).

• Native speakers—Spoken by natives of the country who are language teachers at leading colleges and universities.

• Convenient manual—Contains every word on the cassettes—all fully indexed for fast phrase or word location.

Each boxed set contains one 90-minute cassette and complete manual.

Listen & Learn French . . . . .Cassette and Manual
99914-9

Listen & Learn German . . . . . . .Cassette and Manual
99915-7

Listen & Learn Italian . . . . .Cassette and Manual
99916-5

Listen & Learn Japanese . . . . . . .Cassette and Manual
99917-3

Listen & Learn Modern Greek . .Cassette and Manual
99921-1

Listen & Learn Modern Hebrew Cassette and Manual
99923-8

Listen & Learn Russian . . . . .Cassette and Manual
99920-3

Listen & Learn Spanish . . . . .Cassette and Manual
99918-1

Listen & Learn Swedish . . . . .Cassette and Manual
99922-X

Precise, to-the-point guides for adults with limited learning time

ESSENTIAL GRAMMAR SERIES

Designed for independent study or as supplements to conventional courses, the *Essential Grammar* series provides clear explanations of all aspects of grammar—no trivia, no archaic material. Do not confuse these volumes with abridged grammars. These volumes are complete. All volumes 5⅜" x 8½".

ESSENTIAL FRENCH GRAMMAR, Seymour Resnick. 159pp. °20419-7 Pa.

ESSENTIAL GERMAN GRAMMAR, Guy Stern and E. F. Bleiler. 124pp. °20422-7 Pa.

ESSENTIAL ITALIAN GRAMMAR, Olga Ragusa. 111pp. °20779-X Pa.

ESSENTIAL JAPANESE GRAMMAR, E. F. Bleiler. 156pp. 21027-8 Pa.

ESSENTIAL PORTUGUESE GRAMMAR, Alexander da R. Prista. 114pp. 21650-0 Pa.

ESSENTIAL SPANISH GRAMMAR, Seymour Resnick. 115pp. °20780-3 Pa.

ESSENTIAL MODERN GREEK GRAMMAR, Douglas Q. Adams. 128pp. 25133-0 Pa.

ESSENTIAL DUTCH GRAMMAR, Henry R. Stern. 110pp. 24675-2 Pa.

ESSENTIAL ENGLISH GRAMMAR, Philip Gucker. 177pp. 21649-7 Pa.

°Not available in British Commonwealth Countries except Canada.